beached rd.

also by neil paech

the bitumen rhino
k is for keeper a is for – t.v.
the skinscape voyeur

no. 14 friendly st. poetry reader (co-editor)

acknowledgements

books and magazines
the friendly st. poetry readers
overland
oxford book of animal poems (anthology)
the phoenix review
poems for trains and buses
the southern review
rattling in the wind (anthology)
tuesday night live (anthology)

source
alexander tolmer, *reminiscences*

readings
adelaide writers' week
beat route, the cargo club
boltz
grace emily
the loungeroom poets, la mama (fringe, '94)
new writing performed, club foote
the railway family hotel, gawler
spoken writ, the crown and anchor hotel
tapas
writers' field day, mt. barker
5MMM
5UV

beached rd.

neil paech

Wakefield
Press

Wakefield Press
1 The Parade West
Kent Town
South Australia 5067
www.wakefieldpress.com.au

First published 2006

Front cover painting by Michael Constantinou
Cover and text designed by Clinton Ellicott, Wakefield Press
Typeset by Ryan Paine, Wakefield Press
Printed and bound by Hyde Park Press, Adelaide

National Library of Australia
Cataloguing-in-Publication entry

Paech, Neil.
Beached rd.

ISBN 1 86254 667 3.

I. Title.

A821.3

Publication of this book was assisted
by the Commonwealth Government
through the Australia Council,
its arts funding and advisory body.

'i am completely normal. even when i
was carrying out the task of extermination
i led a normal family life.'

– rudolf hoess, commandant of auschwitz

nothing happening
but a series of minor events
trivia on the loose

the blonde
her legs like whips in jeans
back towards me
and kicking junk into the gutter
of her lawn
before her house yanks her back inside

that anaemic alsatian
nosing around the fresh grass
for something intangible

a kid racing his bike along the pavement
and tugging a string held one-handed
while trying to scoop air into a plastic bag
and mostly failing

another complaining
that he can't stop the water
as a trickle trickles along the gutter
and through his fingers

shoppers trying to force themselves
to buy a packet or can of something or other
to keep them interested

the gums soggy and without their galahs
because the air is humourless
and barely bearing to carry themselves

outersuburbia seeming forever
no terror that time has stopped
bleached of emotion

that every decent-sized event has been cut up
into a series
of minor casualties

grazed knees on gravel and asphalt

can you hear me, mate? i want you to come out without the firearm. i
want you to come out now. to work it out

   the aluminium body cruises king william st.
      blank skins stripped off faces
      blurt out words that fall
      to asphalt/
                splintered tinsel
lips/& hands/dentures/toes/erections
hair/periods/of pain
     tow & rattle along behind the bus
     like cans tied to a honeymoon car
a head falls off/rocks & rolls towards its destination/
         a cock/a cunt

   the town hall rises into the night
   a clock churns away on the cock/3 sides
   for voyeur participation/black hands
      that wipe over a white face
      & keep time straight
            if time stops
            the tower subsides
            & the govt. falls

         every major city in australia has one

   a punk dances at a party
   with a rifle slung over his back
   & dressed in kharki fatigues

a woman seems impressed with the uncertainty of the
                intention
it seems a good line   the violent question-mark
                which dribbles from her mouth

         some woman dances with a queen
         he zips her up
         she flashes thick red lips
         a red dress
         plenty of pink gum

i don't believe in objectivity
i do believe in everything being visual

                                     & if you believe in exploitation
                                     first show me the victim/
                                                     or non-victim

i can't find a morality of good & bad
in this closet of make-believe

                                     only power exists
                                     & your ability to make everyone
                                     believe you're right/
                                     your way is the successful way
                                     to survival

some people eat heads
some people eat testicles
some don't eat at all
the winner survives to burn your theories
to ignore them or accept them
                               at a whim

                         a humiliation is being the subject
                         of someone else's whim/chains on the hands
                                                       & mouth

all these faces eating spiced chicken leg
licking their lips over
& you can't tell who's a homosexual/bisexual/heterosexual
                       you can't live by voice alone

the toilet as a place to meet graffiti
shake hands with yourself
& clothes/
                       clothes are only an indicator
                       sometimes

                                               skin & hands
                                               across a sea of urine

masturbating up the arse

                                    a red tail-light on a bike
                                    ridden by a girl
                                    with tight hips & jeans
                                    rubbing herself away
                                    on the rhythm of the seat/
                                                she rides herself

hands are handsome

        the breakers clean the abortions away
        from the area near the can-openers

            you expect me to be objective
            about sighting a cock & balls coming at me
            like a U.F.O. rising into the sky/lights flashing/
            engines rattling
            like a cheap pinball machine
            after scoring the big number
            with a cheap 20c coin
            easy come easy go

sucking off my father's cock
& wondering if he can get it up any more

                        biting off the chicken skin of the chicken leg
                        & finding a cock to nibble
                        delicately

                        the cheese dip a brand of semen
                        from the waterfront docks/the ship's
                        come in

            post-war

                                pre-ground/background

*at eight o'clock this morning saw the dray off for the purpose of
picking up the boat which was to be pulled down the south-eastern
branch of the waterway by a party of shadows, the only crew i could
muster*

how do you raise
          a limp prick
                    from the dead?

          soft sausage into tough gristle/point the bone/raise
superman off the bed like bread?

                              bake a meat roll
          from lethargy?

by applying electrodes to
          genitals
                    electric shock treatment/forget amnesty

          sleeping zipped up in a tongue for sleeping bag
          a huge tongue
                    rasping up the whole body
                         licking off
                    like rough water
                              lapping away at
                                   the banks
                         a flood of rough tongue

throwing on ice
to solidify effort into icicle
          cutting out the bends
                    from trying to rise too quickly
                              from too deep down

                         slapping cement on
                         your hands as trowels
                         building a building
                         brick by brick
                              to create
                              a rock
                                   of sand

a tongue like a sleeping bag
          & dressed to kill
                    glass lips
                         a rubber mouth

                                              blowing up meat balloons
        trying to look like
              a horse

moving a cunt up close
all that carpet to vacuum
grass to mow
        trying to enjoy outersuburbia & the mortgage & 9 to 5

trying to raise a rise
        plenty of effort
              a matter of resurrection of the past/try again
                                        like the
                                              spider
                        building a web/connection
                              inch by inch

whips & black leather
              rita hayworth stripping off that long black glove
                              the arm straight & hard
                                    as gliding gilda
                                    (hit & run/
                                        hit & run)

        erect breasts/cold nipples   the cold stare
              through silk

        sharpening a lead pencil with hands

trying to push it up the hill
magnetise that hill
                        that mountain of muscle & blood
              trying to get it up/
                        meeting the gardener/
                              digging up the skin
                                    with a shovel
              stroking footsteps
                        dragging a log up   working it up

walking it like a dog on a leash   walking up
                                              to running
                                        an erection

6

                              like an election
                              like tap water
                              in a bath   /thick
                                             & long
                                             & strong
                                             & relaxing

                        are you going to acknowledge
me? can you hear me? i want you to come out, mate, and put the
firearm down. no-one will do anything. i want you to come out and
talk to me so that i know you're there

the window is the complete rationale
for morning
we only receive the meaning of morning
through the window
                    & the odd bird remaining invisible
                        behind its sound
                    & the vine leaves
                        filtering a yellow sky into a gradual steady
                        transigence

green vine leaves green vine leaves green vine leaves green
morning

meryl streep is a mediocre actress with no steel & concrete
below her softness/her upper middle class play-acting/
her endorsement of the bourgeois & the sentimental
she is blancmange
all she has is a white face
america is sentimental about its exploitation of the 3rd world
inside its own heart/its lungs cough with sentimentalism
it stands & applauds meryl streep like their anthem

            it came on to blow fresh from N.W., and gradually
increased, so much so that on shoving off i found the shadows, with all
their exertions, made no headway

the dumb-quiet magpies sledge the ground
with their beaks

for them the world is black and white still
simple as that

rainbows are black and white

they're pieces of a black and white rainbow

i want you to put the rifle down. put the rifle down and come out of
that shop. come out of the shop, mate. i can see you and i want you to
come out of that shop. come out of the shope, mate

a czech refugee with no knowledge of english/australian
& still living at the hostel
performs acts of carpentry on marianne's bookshelves
i avoid looking at his face
he has a pregnant wife soon to grow a baby outside of her
he needs extra cash
he works sign language into shelves where marianne will place
her legs & arms & head after she's read them

> with her head broken off her neck she'll lie in bed & read
> them as they prop the wall up like ornaments/her imagination
> on display

claire is making paper bricks outside at 10c a pop/ the
incentive of capitalism/money & the dream of buying purchasing power

marilyn monroe's face/black & white desires/dots of teeth/
eyes/lips/hair/nostrils/creases crossing through her forehead
& nose & lower lip

> & birds hiding behind the sound of colour
> & singing behind the colour of sound

& hanging in the air by its fingertips the image
of her body/her legs whipped clean right down to the
muscle by the grate & its updrafts lifting her skirt
out & up to her white pants/panties & joe dimaggio's seething

inside with jealousy & believing in his mathematical
emotions/calculations that she should be his property alone
& not the viewpt. of those pimple-faced cameramen
with rods of steel & millions in the audience across the
country/cuntries of the world & a thousand & one machines
with tongues of iron & eyes of steel

& the morning light is a white colourless hole behind
black grape leaves & the room is black with blank &
one leaf a spotlight of sickly green-yellow &
another leaf somewhere else & more leaves & several
more & more & more & black retreating fast/slow/faster
& ferns in the room turning a dark green/& their ladders
showing light & the brown stains on the edge of leaves becoming
an apparent fact & the chimney behind the building behind
the leaves a red brick & the black retreating to the vine branch
& the sky a white light like an angel's wing
burning with leprosy/the sound of an airliner passing
                    is really the sound of feathers burning

        lapping up diarrhoea out of a dog's bowl

at first i intended taking only two shadows, but hearing that there was
another who had been far down the eastern branch, i included him in
the party. by eight the boat was loaded, when we started with a good
breeze from the N.W., following the channel to southward of the isle

        i don't know
        how many horses you saw in your lifetime
        let alone patted
        how many words you read
        backwards

        i don't know how many times
        you turned your head to the north
        to look for that overheated north wind
        currying clouds south

i don't know how many plates
you picked up
and dropped
how many forks you put to your mouth

i don't know how many roads
you started to cross
then changed your mind

i don't know how many words
you spoke
and who refused to listen

i don't know how many makes of cars you drove
and their colour

i don't know

all i know are scraps

as soon as i walked in the kitchen
my mother told me the news
as if she'd cooked me up one of her favourite dishes

someone hadn't seen you for two days
and when they investigated
they found you deader than a clichéd doornail
on the kitchen floor
caught out while cooking vegetables
the doctor had advised you to eat everyday
because you were being run down by death
after living alone off and on for 7 pedestrian years

you'd tried several relationships
my mother said
since your wife died
but they'd never worked out

maybe you'd been dead a day or two
but as to the state of your decomposition
and the kind of tyre mark running up your back
from the cartoon show of your dying
my mother couldn't say
she hadn't foraged out that much information as yet

they went to your funeral the other week
a giant one for springton
because you were so well known
83, you'd had a good spell
my mother said
the second of the boys to go
only one left
she said
and you gave my mother a chance
to see her hometown and sisters again
be a star again
which she didn't say

i don't know whether the vegetables boiled dry
and your saucepan is an unwashable black scab now
but i'd somehow like to know all about the details of this
your last act of fire at leaving

i don't know what you looked like
don't even know whether i ever met you
even as a baby

what i do know
is that you were the black sheep of my mother's family
and she always used you in family discussions
on family untogetherness
and over the years
as i found myself hedged and clipped into that role myself
i identified you more and more in myself

you were a teacher
i became a teacher
and we both used our books to read ourselves out
of the provincialism and small-townisms of our respective families
both preferring the new york of people massaging people

i don't even know whether we would have liked each other
if we'd actually met
but i didn't have to meet you to like the way you drove
and i'm sorry now we never met
outside of other people's words

but my imagination still carries you
and it's no coffin

i do know you were known as uncle ed
carried the name of a half-hour b-grade american comedy series on t.v.
about a talking horse
but even that seems wryly appropriate
for you were born in 1900 and kept pace with the C20th
you were born with horses and died with cars
one of history's elite
starting off with all 4 feet on the ground
and ending up in an age of footsteps rocketing across
the vacuums of space

and the last thing i know about you
was that your last trip anywhere was in a car
followed by a calvary of cars
and your power over everyone was a measure of horse-power

for the first time the C20th is going to feel older than you
who it's tried to leave behind for a long time now
as an anachronism
perhaps now it can relax with its exhaustion

for i don't know how many times you went to war
with others and yourself
how many times you declared a truce
or whether it was one interminable 83 yr war
all i do know is that it wasn't peace

so many things i don't know about you
so many things now i'll never know

what was your favourite colour, ed?
mine is red

come outside, mate. come out without the firearm. we want you to.
okay, mate, come outside without the firearm. come out, mate, so we
can talk to you. we want you to come out, mate, without the firearm,
and have a talk. i want you to come out and put your firearm down. i
want you to come out

& kurt raab asking if the jacarandas outside the cinema
('this tree') as he touches a leaf are evergreens
   & if it ever snows in adelaide

    & fassbinder booking a ticket on the cockcorde to new
york & back & writing the script for querelle of brest
on the flight
      driving a wedge between the directors & producer
so he'd get the directorship   because he'd read the book at 15
                            & said then he'd make a film of it
                            one day

      200 pages of voice-over dialogue
      & raab brought in by the producers to rewrite
      the script in 3 days/& have a translation in fr.
      ready to be sent off to france to the co-fr. producer
      & 2 scenes of heterosexual love having to
      be included in the script for the govt. to fund
      the film/cut out in the actual filming/
      & fassbinder not told the script rewritten until
      the grant had been received/no comment

a group sitting facing a table of guest speaker/
coffee/questions & answers in german/translation
below the monroe face/everything is an appendage
of monroe sex shaking hands & cock with fassbinder

    the guest speaker a chameleon of sex & drugs & bent words
on fire before the pyro audience/matches & sweat &
kerosene conversations
                      oxy-acetylene flames from bums
                          & mouths & cocks
                              & cunts
                  oxy-acetylene thoughts/images/
                            imagination/
                              dreams

    & the leaves are turning a transparent yellow
    & the sky a pastel blue/their veins are visible/
                  their skeletal arrangements

& lithuanian refugees in new york/manhattan &
brooklyn/ demonstrating against the russian embassy
about big nations eating up little nations
           poets & picnics in central park & people talking
without voices/& demos/& peace against the bomb
marches/THIS IS INSANITY/snow & leafletting in
bitter snow & river ice drifting down the hudson weather
& women demonstrating on the coldest day of the yr. in new
york & backs pressed against glass in a sit-in/a mock-
up fall out shelter/& cops on horses & foot

      reminders of my ancestors/political-religious
refugees from silesia in the 1800s

            exiles/hoping to return
            & ovid on the black sea
            & russians outside paris   /the continual
                                    flash-backs & nostalgias

doco's of people & rain in the streets/tenements & the cold
& trying to write in the cold & hitching back to new york/
bodies in the car/bodies outside

            the accident/the dead fingers in the puddle/the voyeur
of death

                  peter, one of the shadows, said he was told that some
of the whites were murdered at a spot on the land side we were now
abreast of. hauled in, landed, and after an hour's search with no
success we again shoved off

their albino faces
sit around the sprung green
the spring garden
no juice
no blood
no wine
no-one to turn the water in their veins

and like dried clots of dirt
they open their blooms to the manufacture
of dust
their teeth false
their puncturing will extracted
old vampires turning to rust
and reflected in mirrors of young nights
when they could scare nightmares
into submission
and now scan-scaring only desultory memories
of deaths and dying back
like noxious plants sprayed
into coffins and thoughts
abstractions without substance

farmstock themselves
genetically misbred to die
they hang on in this outersuburban garden
shorn green bald
so their slowed down feet won't trip up
on any garrulous overwhelming growth
like weeds they're weeds

they hang on
upside down
like bats their lives upside down
the sand running out their veins almost out
fallen to the bottom of their time off/left

and unable to fly back they hang on like white washing
cleaned up cleaned off
the colour of corpses rinsed out of all future

and they wait while they celebrate
the butt-burning turning twisting 70 of one of them
among the memories of heart attacks/
diseased kidneys/black dresses/suits/
war young the always young because/drownings/
cancers/the overturned tractors
– those intimate moments of intercourse
   with graveyards and gods

and they wait among dead chickens
deheaded and hanging from washing lines
dripping blood bouquets

and among the slit throats of calves and other beasts
themselves now the cattled beasts waiting
in barren stockyards for the knives and mallets
of eyes around them

they wait
impassive from a life's herding into submission
the questions of why, when and where unanswered/
always
and left to hang
from their throats and ears and noses
like the chains and rings of bulls
used for a moment's breeding breathing
until the axe fall/clear felling of the dead wood
for profit/the neck opening the head falling
drowning in barbed-wire blood

and they wait
with the lost boat
while fishing the dead companion
unable to make it to shore
through the swimming the fishing
the fish of bloated guilt/christ/resurrecting
to make a haunting of the dead

and they wait
with the aunt shaking white over her son
seen through her nephew/the ghost
of that tractor falling through the killing

these fruit gone yellow close to falling
past open mouths into the black and hungry
the open mouth wide that consumes all garbage
city and country/ they're ready to fall
and their faces show their horror for it of it
as they sip tea eat their cream puffs
with delicacy no cream pouring out the edges
their teeth extra careful

and you can only feel sorry for them
about to go down head down drown in dirt

and there's something cutting sad in
this drought that now rushes their veins
like tidal waves of lovers rioters terrorists
ashes to ashes dust to dust
if the devil don't get you
your god must

                the only way we're going to come to any sort
of agreement is if we talk. tell us who you are. you told the policeman
who got here first 'this isn't a break'. are you going to talk to us? i
know who you are

        the face of a blonde on the wall/straight hair
instead of monroe's wavy bleach
            no teeth visible in the black slit of her mouth
     creases running through her eyes down her cheeks
        like tears
               they would tear easily
    & on the bed at the foot the gangster
who robs supermarkets & the woman
           & later the negro with his arse open
        shot down in a supermarket among the cans/
               a woolworths/not worth it
        a coles/   a cold chilly fire/
                  cold bones/rigor
                        mortis
      a tom-the-cheap/the price is too dear

a mini-skirt/reaching up to pull out the goods/
        everyone has to eat/even the poor/
        mass-produced stomachs/desires/
sex has to be fed from cans/pensioners have sex
with the rough-sawn edges of dog-food lids

   jealousy in the supermarket/legs & thighs detached/p
   lips/cops in the supermarket/crooked lust/sex-killings
   in the supermarket

a shadow pointed out the spot near
which the murder was committed on the coast. we landed

having sex with a car tyre
by allowing it to run over me
starting at the cock
a tyre imprint left on the scene of the crime
a cast taken for future evidence/
the date of the trial to be determined

claire slices an ear off & places it on my mouth/i remain
indifferent

the phone rings/no-one answers it/they'll call back if
it's important

slicing open my father's testicle sacs
scooping out his balls/
like cherries/spitting out the seeds/
like olives/placing the pips carefully
on the paper plate next to chicken bones/scraps
i scoop out his penis filling with my spoon/a biscuit

the place is surrounded. so i want you to answer the phone when it
rings. please answer it when it rings. hullo in there, i would like you to
answer the telephone. the sooner you talk to us the sooner we can
resolve this

crayfish in a restaurant fishtank
like a barbwire of jigsaw puzzles

so much awkwardness

bits of pieces. odds and edges. points
that stick out to beat you with

and at the centre the thickness of them all
as they pile up and over each other

trying hard to locate the slot
to slot into

18

never quite. no hope

the nightmare of a child's id. or an id's
child

a knock-kneed tangle of tumours

the humour
of the half-baked drunk of it all

all over red rover

we had not proceeded far when the middle party hailed us; and on
reaching where they were, the sight i witnessed was truly horrible.
there were legs, arms, and portions of bodies partially covered with
sand. in one place was a body with the flesh completely off the bones,
with the exception of the hands and feet

in a bourgeois home/carpets/2 way mirrors
severed heads/conversations/emotion
counting out money in the toilet/wiping your arse with it/
$50 bills/not used as much/
      masturbating with $5 bills/caroline chisholm

concentrate on the face/always concentrate on the face/that's
where all the answers lie

the leaves have shadows now/the shadows are concrete forms
               with clear edges

    a 'philip' tattoo

              her lips hang down like moss
              she

you won't get hurt. grab the telephone and tell me what you would like
to do. without talking we are going to get nowhere. you inside the
shop, we are not going to hurt you. don't get frightened. you're not
going to get hurt but at the same time if you don't talk to us nothing is
going to be resolved

morning cold weighs in
        & a wagtail darts about some branches
       showing off   it's alive & kicking
kicking up a fuss of feathers
in the face of some despairing maggie
                 just wanting to sit it out
                 yawn the morning off

just a bird
wagtail willy
just a bird
sitting on a fence
        in formal white formal black
      a little hearse dressed up
   head & tail confused machinery
          its tail a jiggling tea-bag
          a packaged movement of tail vibrations
      a little joke in black & white
                a clown
rolling ball-bearings   up & down
            up & down its throat

   cleaning its conscience off
                on iron fences
those ribs around FOR SALE signs, english shrubs,
gums, manicured lawns, brick veneers

   only an ornament on the lawn
harmless garden kitsch

        a diver   a swimmer
        no grace at all
     bum in the air   legs akimbo
       head nowhere & everywhere in particular
       an unpredictable generalisation
             shock & grin
    but no spectator
    evrything's go, go, go

this small confusion of instincts trying out
its promiscuous curiosity   as luck
             anywhere everywhere

one eye sucking the other for echoes

while a white cat hunches
its eyes radar
& creeping closer towards its stomach
a smile trying a street   a pick-up
                                           a casual affair

saliva rolling an eye over

            & as if playing its own ego
            wagtail dancing the lawn
                  flying at a lower window
                        attempting a dive
                        into the glass reflection of trees

& for a moment
the dream seeming more perfect than reality
the correct route to follow

                  but having time to recorrect

the kaurna knew this tattle-tale
as bad luck
a spreader of secrets

& they fell off the edge of the world
were shoved

& now the wagtails are the scraps left over
the flying bones & whispers
                              like black words
                              on white paper

i took no side
willy says
i took no side
                  you can't confuse me accuse me
                  not just because
you did it
            i didn't
                  you did it `
                              i didn't

& like our black & white conscience
the wagtail now flirts about our gardens
just keeping out of the way of being mowed & mulched

the wagtail is a memo from the past
of how the past digests our future
gives it a sour edge

                    like a leaf
                    that's hacking into autumn

that look & taste of death
that salt & pepper

                  that makes us realise
reality is always just around the corner
(& about to catch us up
 for back taxes

all tracks were completely obliterated, with the exception of a few
tracks of shadows, and those very faint, and there were no signs by
which we could trace from whence they came

        on the bus
        his lines have trapped weather
        analysed it/dissected it/run it down catchment creeks
        & gullies into his mouth from his forehead
          into his eyes
          down his cheeks
          around his chin
                  gorges & clefts/cliffs
                  people have been killed on his face
                  by falling in/falling down
                  mountain climbers traverse
                  light fires in his skin among the win
                  that howl away down their throats
     a woman mutters in a critical accent at the bus driver
     she distracts him/he misses a pensioner holding up a blue
              pension card/leaves him to feel rejected/to blow
                          away

leaves yellow with puss & a vomit of light
    light vomits

                cold sores

    please answer the telephone when we ring you up and
make a proposal. come on, talk to us. come on, talk to us. all we want
to do is talk. talk to us

the sea is all around me.
it is telepathic and consummates
my perseverance

i am a weather machine
that manufactures rain in eyes
and wind in skin

i listen to the whales sing.
they are the conscience of the sea.
they are the chimera of youth

i watch cows eat seaweed on the beach
and chase them

they are rocks that run and fogs with mouths
that paralyse words

there is a fog all around me
and the sea is that great lonely sea-cow
that breathes down hard on the back of my neck.
i can hear its hungry heartbeat
as it follows me

i listen hard for the breathing of rocks

there is too much fog in the whales' singing
and they lure me

         then landed, and proceeded over the
beach; at eleven we reached the wreck, and from it saw several
shadows a-head of us. we tried hard to get up with them, but they
must evidently have seen us, not allowing us to near them. at last we
gave it up

regards from wainer
                 you have to act expressionistically

          this is a colour film
                      but i'm really shooting it in black & white
                                        /said to the cameraman

he hated anything happening accidentally
          /hated improvisation

'a cunt of a film'/why does m.r. run amok?

     he lived in a cage so big he couldn't even see the bars

open-ended

              if you don't talk to us i'll have to send in a police
dog. or send someone in. unless you talk to me on the telephone. there
are people wanting to go to work. i can't afford to let this go on much
longer. people want to go to work. i'll have to send in a police dog. it
won't do you much good and i don't want to do it

                    sitting next to this woman i know in the cinema
                    & that attraction beating at the door
                    of the palms & eyes/that crinkling of
                    the skin/what's her name? what's her name?
                    churning thru my mind, too tired to think,
                    when did i last remember her name anyway,
                    her boyfriend's name is/was tom.
                    she's usually with him/not with him tonight/
                    what's her name/all i can think of is maggot/
                    an anti-name/too tired to think

                        in crossing over to the boat, on
reaching the summit of a slight eminence just below us i saw two
shadows. the moment they saw us they set up such a yell of fear that the
shadows who were with us and were a little behind, were rather startled

24

addiction to nicotine/the right hand the only thing
moving on the body lying on the couch/lighting a cigarette before
the other is finished/the bloated body
          lying on a bed on the floor/sex mags lying nearby/
sheets of script/pills/sleeping pills & drugs beating in
the system/the director lying next door/not putting thru a ph. call
from the ex-wife who had a feeling/his current girl back from
a drinking binge/listening at the door/the t.v. humming/no snoring/
autopsy

      at the theatre/his pimply face poking in a door/
        at the cinema/3 films a day-on-the-cheap/
food between/mother a translator
        his rejection by film school/not finishing high school/
        parents splitting up

in spain. car driving thru an intersection/ they would have been
killed if . . . . /kurt raab not wanting to die/
          after kicking a woman on the cast
                being beaten up by 2 sp. electricians
          on the set as the others watch/
    his mulatto boyfriend/trying to buy him with presents/a car
etc/married/uncertain/being given a main acting role/won over/
        the use of cherubs in set work/a cross/the catholic influence

        2 women used to raise money by fucking foreign workers
as he writes his script across the st./used as pros. as reward
          in a later film

      the woman actor who was vegetarian/he'd fuck her
as many times as steaks she ate. she ate one/
vomited in the toilet/he refused   . . . if she ate it/didn't vomit

*you in there. i did ask you to handle the phone. answer the telephone,
please. when the telephone starts ringing pick it up. just walk across
and pick it up. the phone is ringing again. walk over and pick it up and
talk to me. i would like you to talk to me. tell me what you actually
want. come out through the back door. that's all you have to do and we
can all go home*

              life is precious   the negro said
                                        as he shot the woman down
                                        & then fell to the floor of the toilet (himself)

                        after reaching the boat a small party of
        shadows made their appearance, and their information perfectly agreed
        with that given by the other two

              the scrub was cleared a hundred yrs or more ago
              and only a low brick wall and a mesh-wire fence
              now surrounds the perimeter
              of these old men in white uniforms bowling down
              a score of HFC vs VISITORS
              white numbers against a black background

              and the neutrality of the sea of lawn
              is a perfect calm. no roughness to disturb
              their concentration. their emotions played out
              on a linear surface with bias

              a white ball sails from one end
              of their world to the other
              repositioning their emotional centre

              and then the bias of their argument
              over landing rights begins
              the black balls tortured with an unhurried twist
              into a measurable definition around the white

              a shadow tries to outrace each ball
              as it rolls toward a dead stop
              never quite makes the break

              and an occasional black ball casualty
              rolls off the end
              into the gutter
              too far gone under the influence
              of a heavy hand
              among the quips about too much to drink
              by these casual old men

who carry their emergencies only skin-deep
a bent knee
a wave of a hand
a crease

each game is merely a change of end
the basics the same
only the depth of hope and despair
a shallow fluctuation

while
above them
an airliner spears irredeemably up across the sea
after take-off
its overseas flight a launching back
into tourist heaven
where nothing is too serious to be ignored

come on, you in the shop, speak to us. talk to us. speak to me. talk to us

a mosquito lurks around me
as i lie in my sleeping bag
to taste my blood/suck
mosquitoes that drink blood are always female

a man is someone with balls & a cock
a woman someone with a cunt & breasts
a human being has none of these identity discs

*on just arriving at the camping place,
it being nearly dark, a great many shadows made their appearance, at
the same time keeping at a respectful distance. it was dark when we
landed*

an eclectic interest in all music/beethoven to 50s
sentimentalism/to new wave 'dada'/
his girlfriend thinking she should honour him at his funeral
by playing all the music he loved/it went on for 4 hrs
& many people left after a half-hr or so/they couldn't stand it

picking a person up & placing it inside
the image of that person/box within a box/
placing it inside/pulling it out/placing it inside
several times

another male lover from algeria with kids/taking them to france/
leaving him eventually & hiding in motel rooms/the male lover, kemal,
going berserk/stabbing several people/being hustled onto a plane
for france to escape the cops by friends/wandering europe
& selling drugs/hanging himself in a fr. prison cell/
fassbinder indifferent

another lover/rejected, he killed himself in a shared apartment/
in the kitchen

raab on a television contract/fassbinder telling the t.v. station
he wants him for a new film/the contract voided/outside,
raab told there's no new film as yet

'you're a bourgeois'

his urgings of raab to take cocaine to extend his acting/
eventually doing so & becoming addicted/his ration cut back/
taking it secretly from places where it was hidden/
looking out a window at snow falling/*good friday*/
& leaving in a flurry of snow

fassbinder writing a script at a casino in the bahamas
among the jangle of machines
on a rough road through mexico
on the new york docks for a week or so/the bars/fassbinder
the voyeur/watching

raab his 'enemy' after he'd left him
– invited to dinner parties as 'his enemy'

the hostile comments:
'if you want to see your friends you'll have
to go to prison.'
'if you want to see yours
you'll have to go to the cemetery'

the pale look on the face/
                    regretting the comment

his sweats, when meeting his mother
                    the formalities/rituals established/greetings/
                                        'mütter'

        the coldness

                            now i told you if you don't talk to
me i'm going to have to send in a couple of dogs. i'll have no alterna-
tive. if you don't talk to me i'll have to send the dogs in. make up
your mind pretty smart. are you going to talk to me or do i send the
dogs in?

        at 77 he stands there like the fag end of a rag
        a washed out specimen on a hook
        bone shoulders and red gutted face
        a projecting belly and trousers falling from his hips in disarray
        like wasted lips off no tomorrow.
        the idea of the bag is definitely in
        and someone is giving a dedication to him at the podium
        the crowd crowding in on them in a semi-reverent semi-circle
        he the strawberries oysters and fr. champagne
        of their attention. but his mind is indifferent
        his eyes spiralling off on the back of a black and white magpie
        out for a stroll on the lawn between them. neutral ground.
        a somewhat bedraggled and intent bird
        arrogant with that long-legged strut and shuffle
        that produces the magic of the worm in the end
        from the hat of the ground
        picking it up on prodding at it
        thrusting at it with vicious jerks and severs
        until it disappears down the plughole of that one last time.
        a worm is the ultimate in dedications
        and a bird has the last word

*after breakfast we shoved
across to the sandhills, where there were a great many shadows
assembled in separate groups. many of them had blankets and pieces
of apparel about them. it was some time before they would come
near us, and even then they invariably threw off what clothing they
had on*

baby, you're a politician
changing offices after defeat
and shredding jill's time and energy
into 3 hr. strips

jill is nothing but breast
and you're all mouth

like mae west peeling a grape
you peel her nipple

you're a sea with a breast like a soggy mattress
bobbing along in the undertow
and fighting for breath

the bogart-bacall movie on t.v.'s a hoax
because you're the real killer
and you're going to get away with it

you've hit your victim over the head with your mouth
as hard as any glass ash-tray
so hard the room's shattered

and bogie doesn't have a hope
against you and your dirty nappies
not exactly silk panties
itching for fingers to play out their romantic film score on

can you imagine bogie setting his mouth
around bacall's nipples
and going slops
after you?

nappies don't dance in step in midnight moonlight
in their arms
when something's dripping
on the dance floor
at their feet

hullo. hullo again. i know you were in the shop yes-
terday trying to buy a gun. you were told you couldn't have one
because you didn't have a licence. now, if you don't understand me, tell
us what nationality you are and we'll get an interpreter. tell us what
nationality you are. unless you let us know what nationality you are, if
you can't understand english very well, unless you tell us what nation-
ality you are we can't get an interpreter

a group of young aboriginals
hunched
by the festival theatre

primary colours of clothing
playing havoc
with my attention

faces heavy-set
and burning to fat

'i don't give a fuck
who'

the label
on the opened beer bottle
standing on the brickwork
amongst them

and the glass

brown like their faces
a pick-axe brand

from the silence of this group of shadows when
questioned respecting the murder, their apparent uneasiness at our

presence, more especially when i began to search the pockets of some coats worn by two of the party, i was confident we were among the guilty parties, and if looks were a sufficient condemnation, there were two who were certainly possessed of such, for without exception, they were the most villainous-looking characters i ever saw

a greek old guy/moustache & stick/wedged in
& apologising for sitting so close

the bus sweeps by a girl at a bus stop/
her look of exasperation & helplessness

people are standing in the aisle

i know you have access to a telephone. then we will be able to resolve it on the telephone and the sooner we'll be able to clear this matter up. you're not helping yourself. we'll have to resolve this soon. people are going to have to go to work

the girl/her dress part of the sofa/trying to break away/
dance away

the automatons/a male & female arrangement of arms
a body slipping to the floor/the clasping male figure
the rearranged hand/arm/& head
the continual conditioning

foreign languages/only the visuals understandable
in a confused sense

the nightclub singer lola/the prostitute singing
the means of production/money squeezing out of cocks
into cunts

bureaucrapts

after many fruitless attempts at gaining information from the shadows, we again shoved off, proceeding through the channel between the islands and sand-hills. at 10.30, we again landed

and walked over to the beach. from one of the highest sand-hills and
with a clear horizon we could see nothing

the blonde with curled hair outside

sitting inside with chris charles/comments about bill
& dinner with him
/the voices in his head

he opens his mouth to speak
& a word rolls out

it grows fur
& talks back to him

he kicks it
& it understands

come on, i know you're there, just tell
us what your name is. don't be frightened, just go to the telephone so
we can talk this matter out. you in the shop, when you hear that phone
ring, go and pick it up. talk to me. go and pick it up. come on, the
phone's ringing. go and pick it up. you talk to me on the other end

the bullet came out your gutz
after entering your back

i remember that last drinking session
at 2 in the morning, alex,
you talking the swear words
because you hadn't the energy
to swear them anymore.
full glasses, empty glasses,
full bowels, empty bowels.
after all, we drink
so we can relieve ourselves

you'd seen the cops
and they arrived just after the shooting

it let the air out
and you hissed like a punctured tyre and tube

no-one knows where the bullet is anymore
but they know where you are,
amongst the clichés
that take us all in the end,
empty us of any originality
we ever laid claim to

they should give the bullet a burial,
it's a part of you,
the most important part now,
your kitsch soul,
your quicksand;
you sank in it, it buried you

it's ironic that you died over a mining claim
after resisting american control so fiercely
– the classic american cinematic cliché

perhaps you saw yourself on the drive-in screen
once too often

      the bus slides along the hill-face
      and the drive-in screen visible from the rd.
      slithers with images
      indecipherable
      people

      the screen elides
      as the black moves over its face
      as the bus moves us towards the edge
      edge-on
      and total eclipse

      i watch obliteration

      behind the screen there is nothing but the black egg
      to crack open
      and suck

*on returning we encountered several shadows, who
did not appear alarmed at seeing us, but followed us to the boat, where
three of them remained until we shoved off. one of them had on a
woman's shawl and his constant answer to our questions as to where he
got it was to point to the beach*

the silent female secretary/white-faced/
the room
                & naked plastic mannequins

        the painting/poster
            of a woman/a male/& his penis

        broken glass in hand
                heels on coffee dishes
        she stands & waits for a phone call

*you there? i'm very
disappointed you didn't answer the phone. if you don't have access to
the telephone, call out. if you don't have access, to let this go on is not
fair. i'll have no hesitation in putting a couple of police dogs in*

after missing the bus/
        other buses still waiting in the st./
chris charles drops me off at marianne's/lights out
        so he doesn't come in for coffee/drives off

the black sound of silence
        punctuated by a car picking up a throaty acceleration
    – an mg?/ tyres squealing/a change of gears/
whining brakes/bird (a starling)/ a high-pitched pitch/
sparrows/my beard on the sheets/fridge
humming/a mosquito/light switch/shower heater
rumbling/conversation with marianne/breakfast dishes/paper
rustling/claire with her doll's head & hair/
                /the body of plastic eaten
a steady hum of traffic/my ears/voices of the old women
from next door/our continual conversation about men &

women/cyril & dave & mike & denise in the house/the t.v. on/
only a few words/booze & drugs/about the fr. & denise's father/
affairs

a blue day

        a bus passes the end of the st./
i'm walking along o'connell st. past bus stops
         & denise picks me up/
    she has to look for a park in the city/
        we part

        the art & meaning of the film/voyeurism
        the darkness the medium of the message
        the dark sts./dark cinema

the leaves of light
    shredded by the dark grubs/
        the parasites of leaves

the weather is as cold as antarctic seal shit

pain is a moon
that swings thru the air
& drops shit on us from a great height

  we lick our lips
  & fingers

  'don't worry about the sound. there's nothing wrong with it
  – the short's a silent'

        12.30, we landed on the sand-hill, this being
the furthest spot we could take the boat. walked over to the beach, and
on looking about, i saw a great many footsteps, the impressions very
faint and imperfect

mark wants to go to sea again

have the sea hire him
for its rhythm's sake
as he stares through the glass on watch
at hours of nothing but his introspection
the spray he rattles

but they say there are younger guys
and he's been out too long

so he works on a city building site
building office blocks into aquariums
which he fills with oceans a room at a time
floor at a time

going up?

and sails across girders the consistency of flat seas
as he looks down on the gravity of shore
where everyone's heavy with staying alive

and a wave of steel hangs its jaws above him
like the moon
swings him in its direction at will
as he obeys its orders down to the last command
as it rears above him
its platforms of waves steps into space
to take a dive from
blood against a horizontal cliff

and the wave
is a frankenstein of force he loves as he falls
upwards

and refuses to sink

                    into a city landscape

_____

                                        hullo again.
if you want to come out, put the weapon down and come down to the
hole and put your hands on the wood at the bottom and i'm prepared
to come over and talk to you

        riding a bike across an intersection
        his body crossed by a garish orange cross
        of plastic/an orange visor/
        bare brown top/floral gaudy short shorts/
        he lifts his arse & tilts & farts

the sts. compose themselves around silent film/
non-dialogue & grey/white figures
that are only occasional. the night
is more permanent

a bus roars through the cinema from outside
with its passenger of sound

an ambulance or fire truck moans past/
it hasn't come for me, i believe
so i partially ignore it

the seat beside me is empty
so i shape it into anyone i want to be sitting there/
whoever i'm comfortable with/excited by/
& so am uncomfortable with

a cripple stands in the doorways
of endless unremarkable rules & rooms

> inside, members of her family
> attempt to make love to themselves/
> forget her

> she moves from room to room
> never stopping

executives look out of their office windows
with rifles
they turn back inside in unison
& shoot their secretaries
& then spend hours dictating shorthand
& urgent memos
   to their corpses

they water down the potplants
with their blood

they ask innumerable questions
& think of their wives & husbands
& wonder what an affair with a body would be like

they wonder if they have the strength to continue in their job/
their relationships

at eight o'clock left the boat with the
doctor, two shadows, and three men, leaving the remainder in charge of
the boat. each of us was provided with a day's provisions. commenced
our walk down the beach

the t.v. brings back memories
of vietnam from the dead
words & phrases & names like
demo & pentagon
kent state university
nixon & kennedy & menzies & gordon & holt
the call-up & the marble
the burning of u.s. flags
moratorium marches
the king william st. – north terrace intersection
the chicago convention of '68
the cops & beatings   more cops more beatings
& soldiers in plain clothes beating away at faces
in king william st.   no cops in sight
& cops without numbers
& blood trickling down faces
& marches with running & walking & anger & frustration
& placards & chanting & sit-downs & horses & tacks &
cop bikes all lined up in a row like black flowers
at their very own flower show
& gas bombs & paddy wagons & arrests & jail & running again
& long hair & short hair
& asio & the cia
& soldiers dying all-the-way
with l.b.j.

& now there are new words & names & phrases & formulae like
darwin & the B-52s
omega & the north-west cape
gippsland

spy satellites & cameras-in-the-sky
the fr. testing the pacific/that not-so-peaceful ocean
pine gap
narrungar
roxby downs & uranium & honeymoon & jabiru
emu field & maralinga
& marches & placards & shouting & chanting & anger
& frustration
& short hair & shorter hair
& reagan & bush &
& missiles & polaris submarines
smithfield
& the americans thinking & we hoping with wishful thinking
they're going to save us from the bombs
& a rain of radiation
with an umbrella
like the english saved india & their empire

& johnson's dead & kennedy & nixon now
but like babes-in-the-wood
we're still hanging onto their umbilical cord
sucking our thumbs
& feeding on bottles of a warmed-up formula
of paranoia
& flying shadows/metal bats like vampires circling above us/
sucking sucking sucking/making suckers of us all
& we're still too scared of our own shadow
& we still can't save ourselves from ourselves

& all these people
still thinking they're going to mark the bomb
when it falls
they'll have time to kick it/handball it/throw it
away
when tackled
thinking they're superman/woman

but superman/woman's an american invention
the all-american nuclear family on permanent honeymoon
post-pill

& the bomb's an american invention
& the nuclear umbrella
& our own naïveté

                                            's an american invention

as we are

                                            /they have our patent
                                            on file

                   put the weapon down and come over to that
hole you went in. you won't get hurt. i promise you that. come on, it
won't take long. come over to the hole you went in

interval. marilyn monroe sits at a table
drinking coffee
& saying the critic has misunderstood
the film. it was about people,
not lesbians. about relationships,
not ethnics

chris charles sits across the table with a male friend/
he asks if i've seen bill.
of course, i haven't

                   at 5.20, we found a well of shadows, and
stopped for the night

red hair. aberrant. the voice and the hand qualify
the approach of the mike to the mouth

i'm just a casual girl that's a woman standing out
in the crowd that plants the bar with weeds

that flower into gossip of that lawnmower that went
that a way with that a one. and who was she(he) anyway

but the next door neighbour's left-hand cousin.
i'm a singer singing red songs on the loose

called blue hearts blue rhythms picking up pieces
of centimetre clocks that turn seconds into kilometres

of lovers just waiting for action to hit their fan.
i'm just a redheaded singer trying to make a go

of being a redheaded singer making out. i'm the way
of the wor(l)d. my lips are the way of my blues

my feet in my shoes. i'm looking for the glass
in the hole in the head which is the art

of the heart. quietly loud me. listen

*put the weapon down and you don't
get hurt. nobody gets hurt. and we can go – go and have breakfast. put
the weapon down. it's not going to be of any value to you. put both
weapons down on the ground and come out. come on. i can see you
there. put the weapons down*

people hang themselves like cattle in rows
& cattle slit their throats with knives
the blood runs & runs & runs/
black. ears are skun/the skin slips smoothly
off their tails/their eyeballs remain/their head is dissected
on the chopping block

a bull talks about its childhood (calfhood) to a cow
it had its penis removed in casablanca
so it could have sex with another bull/
the other bull didn't even write/
rejected it

at the end of all this
rejected & dejected by the uselessness of continuing
to add more anecdotes to its story
it hangs itself with an overdose of sleeping pills

the other bull having sex with the cow
on the floor next to the bed
doesn't even notice

from the one who was in charge during my absence, i learned
that they had been visited by a party of shadows from the southward;
they knew nothing of the wreck, but on following up the coast they saw
a whale-boat, and offered to take him to her, they also saw tracks of
white men leading up the coast directly from her

the hammer humour is the shoe on (in) cement. the plastic tongue
of the foot boot jams down hard on language talk (like flak).
spaces jabber-lick and level-lather each other for out up.
position. (they jostle for position). doubt (pisses) (drops it)
(lays it) on us (onus) (on us) (performs on us) shits fucks on us.
from (lays shit) a great height. the (goal) keeper is here (hire).
the keeper is there. the keeper is no longer dead adrenalin
but the resurrection of the steel steak hand. know no evil.
know no (is) irrelevant. (work is joy) (is) the only compromise is
(i am) left as arbiter. (arbitration is compromise).
survival is the great leveller leftover we all sniff at (it).
(our arses are (great) askers). with our arses. (they are
our askers). give me politics and i'll give you an acrimon()us arse
full of acrimon()us daffodils. i wandered lonely as a crowd
and there i saw a host of (ofs) . . . . of of of . . . .
of what ('s their names) for christ's sake?
daffodils politicians arsehole(s) (and) poets
(they) (are) for what for christ's sake? humour is a shoe in cement.
the plastic tongue tyranny of the boot jams down hard on talk.
(discussion) (dissension). politician spaces jabber and lick
and lather each other up for the right (night) position
to stick it up each other. the keeper is here the keeper is there
– the keepers. long live (die) (remain(der)) the keepers.
the keepers (   ) our machines. machineries (rule) rulers. i ring
and can't get through. i prise open the (a) keeper and ask for
my 30 cents back. plus a packet of fags (to go). (mouth) logo.
mouth ego. oral aural satisfaction. dissatisfaction. guaranteed.
ratchet. ratshit

come over to the door and put
your hands on the ledge and you can come out quickly. come on.

43

come on, put the weapons down. don't be scared. i know you didn't
expect to get caught but you did get caught. we can talk about it. but we
can't talk about it unless you're prepared to come down

this bus ride has been boring & uneventful.
nobody at all would buy this bus ride off me.
i couldn't even give it away/let alone hock it.
i'll have to try another one tomorrow/
there is always hope.
i fear lest i'm being deceived/
am deceiving myself

artificial frost

the light through the blind
is yellow/the bottom half of the blind/
the top is a shaded yellow/
the budgies cringe around their cage
they sound enthusiastic about the sun
or something terrible
this way come

landed where we had left the note with the
shadows, they were all away but one, who brought us the note, which
he had carefully stowed away in a corner of his shelter, wrapped up in
a tuft of grass. from him we learned nothing more

leg. the shadow of the leg between the table
and the chair. the cigarette in the hand

fingers. the shadow between the fingers
and the breath. the breath is an angle

between life and death. the nose opens.
the nose closes. the watch around the wrist

the mouth is an open t.v.. i've heard it all before.
an elbow is an elbow. and the hair creaks down

her face is the colour of quiet milk.
she slowly adds it to her coffee

her words are a transfusion below her skin
of calm aesthetics. they are benign

air is a fragile crescendo of coffee all around her.
she is a formation of it

she sits back and listens to her skin.
it goes with coffee

she is able to distinguish between subtleties of taste
in the coffee of language

and leans slowly towards language
as if balancing her words on the palm of her face

her voice spills over her fingers and down her legs
like a warm vibration

and when she walks she suggests the stirring
of coffee

a cup. a hand. the shadow of a hand.
an outline of makeup. the engine of the face

hair catches a glimpse of an eye. the elbow bends
around the arm. bits and pieces are for free

bits and pieces are expensive

the door opens. the door closes. the face rests on a face.
the face bends in on itself

fingers are corridors for the idea of the face.
the face is a suggestion of the enigma of reaction

reaction is such a subtle gasp

a body manoeuvres inside the body. it is a secret design.
the lips are a radio of soft pain

a voice grunts inside the bone. air is such a narrow edge
to stand on. the air is only partly free

only partly. sometimes

her face is a white moon above her coffee cup

i trace the rim with my fingers as she drinks
and clouds whisper through my skin

a piece falls on my hand as it melts
and i drink in clouds instead of coffee

i taste the salt

*come on. put the weapons down. we
can only do this for so long. the alternatives aren't very pleasant. it's
now half-past 6. people are wanting to go to work. put the weapons
down and come out of that hole. if you have difficulty understanding
what i'm saying, throw something out the door to indicate you're
having difficulty in understanding what i'm saying*

what a terror this act
to be able to see the details of yellow
on beak and feet
that ferocity of colour in flare

it was no tame duck

that yellow
too far off to be seen
when a live flight in fight with the sky
way up when with the ever and never

now a dead birth
this yellow
in close-up

lying the road
playing chicken
not hawk

plumped down by the sky
only a plump for a while

about to be plucked
flattened the thickness of book
by car
then the thinness of page

paper weight paper thin
edging from sight
around the corner of rain and sun and drain
a one way ticket to nowhere
the back of beyond

for here there is
a something has happened
and i look my shoulder
for that something is danger contagious
and curious

and me the thought
how i would hate to be
a book
and illiterate

*i landed at the beginning of the narrow
channel; all shadows away, they not appearing to like our company,
and kept wide of us*

richard sitting in the refec at the end table as he always does
'i can remember a guy
in a slaughterhouse
talking continuously about his childhood
while these cows are being butchered.
that's all i can remember.
i can't remember the title.
i've only seen it once'

'sounds like godard'

the crowd is a cubicle (room)
the crowd is a matchbox/cigarette
the crowd is a telephone/box
the crowd is a brain (skull)
the crowd is an idea (l)

are you there? there's nothing much we can do if you're not pre-
pared to talk. if i don't put the dogs in i'll have to put some gas in.
come on out. if you don't, i'll have to have tear gas put in and that's
very unpleasant

i steal her cunt from her
while she isn't looking

i'm a collector of fine art

i place it in my pocket
and walk the sts. with it

i place a hand in and stroke it
for good luck

i pull it out and lick it
to keep it moist
and prevent it from cracking

i take a bite out.
overnight it grows back
to its previous proportion

it's of mythic quality

it has the shape of a cowrie shell
and when i hold it up to my ears
i can hear it whisper

it whispers of love
and the seas of desire

so today, i've decided,
i'm going back for more

two shadows came to us and said it was not the place, but from their hesitation and wishing not to go away, i was certain they were deceiving us. i asked them to show us the spot, they declined on the plea of its being a long way off

& from the bus i can see the lawns
have been freshly mowed
because the weather is warm & pushy

1 kid beside his father
& facing the wrong way on the seat
yells 'g-day'

sweaty legs of a female runner
muscles as hard as concrete

MADNESS
perhaps FUCK or SUCK
graffiti on the puce bus seat

the bus conks out
& the crowd files out of one double bus
into another. everyone sits exactly & precisely
in the equivalent seats

they've added a new dimension to the bus route
by driving off the main rd. to the hospital
& dropping off the sick

i carry my form to the city
looking for addresses to fill in

you in the shop. put the guns down. put the guns down. put your hands through the hole in the back door. put the guns down. you don't need guns. put the guns down and your hands through the doorway now. we're not going to hurt you but you have to come out

she lost the twins, you know,
they were premature.
it was 11 by the time i reached the hospital

49

and what i remember most
was the silence afterwards in the delivery room
that white silence
like a house full of freshly painted rooms
but no furniture
hollow and cold
every scrape of your foot or clothing magnified
– and she's had a miscarriage since.
i was home with her
and she simply burst like a balloon
the blood streaming down.
i had to pick her up
place her on the bed
take off her pants
clean her up
and then take her to hospital.
you know,
it looked just like a piece of steak
and i placed it in a towel
and then in the rubbish bin.
what else could i do?
my father apparently buried one in the backyard
back in scotland
– so my mother told me –
and now she's pregnant again
sits around at home
moody one moment
up the next
and complains about me when i'm down the pub.
but i say to her
what's a man supposed to do
when you shoot off
to your sister's for days
or sit around here without talking
and wrapped up in your own silence?
she's at her sister's now
and claims i don't understand,
but hell,

what did she think i felt like
and went through
when she was going through all that?
and what's made it worse is
i found out a few months ago
i had a kid.
i was living with another woman before her
and she wanted to end it
so i moved out.
but she was pregnant
and decided to tell me later
only after she'd tossed up in her mind about it
– an 18-month-old girl now –
and i see her each week.
we went to the torrens only last weekend
to feed the ducks
– and those ducks sure are aggressive –
one would have taken her fingers right off
when she was feeding it
if i hadn't picked her up.
but the point is,
i like her a lot,
and that's why i've been telling you
it's me taking the chances,
not you.
you've always been scared of relationships
and that's your trouble:
you should take more chances in life
and put yourself on the line more,
like me.
another
beer?

'the horses should with the greatest care be kept out of sight until the last moment. this may be effected by sending them along the sea-beach, not allowing any to rise the sand-hills

sts.
& the primary yellow crane
lifts itself on one leg to piss on the world/
a black ladder leaps up its legbone in jags
& skyscrapers are crucified/nailed against its lattice/
boxes of cigarettes carrying hundreds/
executives & secretaries are cemented onto ledges
like modern gargoyles

'it was a hundred & 30 inside, it was deafening
everything was covered in grease
but they had an excellent lunch'

should you not be able to succeed in capturing any shadows against whom you can obtain evidence satisfactory to yourself, you will arrange your movements so as to return by the time that your provisions are exhausted'

it's supposed to be summer
but it's raining and blowing outside
like the overwrought insides of a whale's breathing
there's plenty of winter left in it yet
and i can see it through the kitchen window
as it busts up the treetops at intervals
the green and white ornamental
the fruit tree
the dark green evergreen
all imports
of european background
transplanted through generations
of suburban gardens
into this uneasy stillness
that gusts and grunts and bursts into some dance of the crazies
their tops only
on display
parts of them
through the wooden frame of the window

among the grey and shifty rain of the cloud
hustling
hustling

and it's sumiji's birthday today
and he's far from where he was born
another land
another dirt
for roots to hold and twist in
like a child's club hands in skirt
other trees
other wood
and his head blobs and bobs by the window frame
as he prepares his japanese pancakes
his head not quite wood
not yet
another type of texture altogether in his dream
as we prepare to eat the results of rain
and the importance of pain
in the heartwood of him

softly now. softly

put the gun down and your hands through
the door. come on. now's the time to do it. put the guns down and your
hands through the door. you got in easy enough, you can get out the
same way

i feel like a bunch of meat
treading water
i feel sliced & lopsided

a bitter weight hangs around
my shoes

i will eat them one day
out of self-spite
in-grown pity
i feel like a bucket of meat

walking around inside myself
on my arm
& no parachute to keep from
        i feel like

i want to boil the saucepan lid
like sex into a kitchen sex act
      kiss
        hiss all over the hot-plate
         & weld my shouts all open

i live too flatly
& am desperately afraid
of dying too flatly
  inch by inch
  of being too alluvial

  (does the fact that)
  there's no such thing as a perfect vacuum
(mean)   i ∴

and it was late in the day when we formed camp among the sand-
hills, in which, fortunately, we found some excellent water in a well of
shadows and plenty of grass of a coarse kind, which nevertheless the
horses seemed to like

the correct party line for the optimist to follow

well,

portrait 1 of a 20th politician

and

portrait 2 of a 20th politician

more

portrait 3 of a 20th politician

money

employed

with

unemployed

with out

the correct party line for the pessimist to follow

but

                           *we were quite happy to talk to you. you didn't
want to talk to us. put the guns down and come out. i told you in the
shop, put the guns down and come to the doorway. i told you you
wouldn't be hurt. put the guns down and come to the door. now is the
time to do it. i know you're there. i know you can hear me. come out*

        cats caterwauling
        the swell of their growling whine
        rising & falling
        waves
        troughs & crests heading in
        towards some beach waiting
        in the blackness/the blankness
        of blind eyes

        staking out territory it's called
        with noise & hackles
        fur bristling
        skin disturbed
        the night sweating darkness all over

        unable to control its bowels
        the night haemorrhages

        going in head first/you have to
        pissing on anything to leave your scent & mark
        & hoping you'll end up with all the fucks you want
        won't have to compromise too much
        with that other bunch of noise & effort

if necessary you'll fertilise the garden
with pieces of
skin & bone & fur
& no regrets

if lucky

that's what it's all about
– being lucky

in consequence of the two live sheep having had their legs tied,
when the boat got adrift they were drowned; their two shadows,
however, which had been killed for immediate use were quite fresh and
good, and none the worse for the soaking in salt water

& in the morning i can feel the yellow light
    thru my eyelids
    even though they're closed
& the sounds of the budgerigars are
    twisted & curled like wood shavings
    tight-fisted & bunched & intricate & precise
    like carved chinese ivory balls
    one inside each other inside each other
    inside each other inside each other

under the pressure of time
i'm unable to fill in my form with addresses
because old men have the newspapers/i have
to wait out my frustration. a bull
i paw the dust from the ground/it floats/
lathers my back/places a curtain between me &
reality (realism)

put the weapons down and come to the doorway and to
the light. you can see the light, come to the light

i remember my mother
as a cold, hard fact

she pursued me
across the dream
across the drama
of being the third act
in a four act play
of children
in a strict lutheran farmhouse
of cows without end,
Amen

she used to run
from the bathroom outside
through the kitchen,
dripping her sex
onto the linoleum

mornings
she'd assiduously read
the obituary column
of the newspaper
to see if she was still alive,
and if she saw someone else's name down she knew
she'd act depressed
but be quick off the mark to tell:
for us
there was always an air of excitement
surrounding dying

in her world of vacant sex
she'd read billy graham's hot words
down the irrigated pasture
while watching the cows graze,
a barbecue of summer shade
under pines.
his words
were acts
of circumcision
sewing up the flaps
of her sex and conscience,
cotton and needle

keeping her locked away
from herself
and shut tight against the wind
that carries the seeds
of the purple-flowering thistles.
she threw his words at herself
like she threw stones
at the cows,
his words
an electric fence
that shocked her back
inside her religious parameters

i used to have sex with my bible,
one chapter a night,
used to fantasise
about sex
with her,
trying to sort out my confusion.
country boys are supposed to know
but you don't see too many cows and bulls
in the missionary position
and having sex with her
could have meant saving myself the embarrassment
of making a fool of myself
with a girl
when it counted,
i thought,
but i couldn't talk to her
through the armour-plating gristle and bone
of her religion

i never did quite figure it out on my own,
and so you can imagine
the brutally embarrassing relationship
i had with myself
that night
i lost my virginity:
it was all fumbles

and naked surprises,
a rude awakening
when i was already awake

there was no way
i was going to ask
'did you like it?'
when i still wasn't sure what
it was all about,
and i was afraid she was going to ask
'how did YOU like it?'
but i was pretty much afraid
she knew already

well, in the next few years
i managed to graduate in more ways
than one
and straighten out my sex act;
i still remember my mother
who's still alive
and those early years
which are still alive:
i'm still living with her

she still wears her bible around her neck
like some black albatross
and i still don't talk to her about sex

*no shadows were seen by either party during the day, although signal
fires were frequent*

the gum leaves
wreathes
of blue smoke
some children probing
and prodding at them
as an adolescent gum
smooth with an adolescent's skin
dawn grey

tall
and bullet straight
wrestles
against a rope
the constant nagging tug of it
while another neighbour
hacks away
with a chainsaw
the gum managing to hold out
for a short time
while the saw is roughly manipulated
from side to side
the top swaying
off-balance
toppling
and tripping the other male
into a hole
but missing him
only flattening the grey
corrugated iron fence
in association
the kids yelling
and clambering over it
like ticks
the males strutting around
like self-congratulatory bulls
on heat
and the next day
the two sheets of corrugated iron
nailed back up
and the fence fixed

don't think about it, come on out now. come on, come to the door. put the guns down and come to the doorway. come to the door. come to the light

you

are a loner already

as you ride the belly your mother the whale
who carries your mouth towards you

the doctor says no to crowds
so you hate crowds already
hitler grand finals football rallies and supermarket intersections
with their chorus line dance productions

there's only room for one pair of shoulders in your mood
your's

you're against sex unless it's you
so your mother has to sail you against the wind
alone

as you stay below decks
learning to play your own special brand of patience

you play yourself to see who'll win

yourself or you

playing out your role of explorer in the antarctic abyss
swinging on your rope thread from a sled that wedges open
the lip
as you gradually pull yourself
up
hand
over
hand

it's a slow trip for all of us

and even if you make it to the top in your fight to the light
you'll be a flop down in your hero alone
unconscious of your journey through pain

and all you'll have at the end of it all
will be a ready acceptance an open mouth two hands
and a fresh start

though that should be enough even for you
i hope

if you make it

about midday we observed a number of shadows
along the coast, two or three miles ahead, and at once gave chase. as
we neared them they took to the sandhills, which rise in that locality to
a great height

she reads the skin of an apple. it tells her
that movement lies on the periphery of things

every time she opens her mouth to speak
she hears the shadow of an echo translated into breathing
inside of her

and like an architect of cloud she hesitates

i stand by the photocopier
and observe her through the slatted blinds
of a window

the window is the frame of her face is a window

outside the library there is nothing
but substance. inside
there is nothing but language

somewhere between them lies hypothesis

put your weapons down. come on, it's not going to get any
better. come on, you won't get hurt. just come out through that hole.
come on, come out through that hole

a bus roars past along the road
beneath the window
a constant traffic noise
as the german marilyn monroe speaks

62

we close the window those extra few inches

the noise filters thru the glass
& she talks of german cinema/
'the arsenal' & avant-garde films/
of pasolini expressing his fury
by intercutting film footage of current political events/
she talks about the poem of faces
he's cut into a mesh of tortured love

what is love?/its consistency?/
how thick/how thin/
runny/or tired/clear/fogged up

how do i distribute myself around emotion?/
i am not pure narrative/or skin/
below the surface lurk angels of monsters/
murderers of lovers in love with the love of murder/
my face is a bus/my teeth axes/
a rat runs around my brain
& stops to eat only occasionally/
it exhausts me with its energy

pasolini is dead & i wish he was back

people break down my face & enter it/
dangerously/part of the sound distorts
& my face blows up/bloated
with too much/the need to cut pieces off/
diet with a knife/flenching flesh

i have filled in my form with ticks of no's & yes's
empty white boxes filled in with ticks & addresses/
       i have run out of time to take it in

        a truck crashes over bumps in the asphalt
        & its iron tray bounces

upon reaching the summit of one of the sand-hills,
i perceived a group of shadows running to conceal themselves in
a thicket at the bottom

denise says working at the golf
club restaurant with brian & je
nny reminds her of herself & ed
ouard: just the way they work q
uietly together without arguing
, talking about whether one of
them's ordered the flowers, pai
d the butcher, the way they sit
relaxing over a cup of coffee &
talking, quietly

it's the first time she's worke
d in a restaurant since they sp
lit up. she cut her meat & thou
ghts up so vigorously & quickly
today she finished early

& then when turning down a st.,
she met edouard & maggie turnin
g in off the main road. she hop
es they don't think she was che
cking on them by driving past t
heir house: she'd been checking
on the leaflets she delivers

edouard hadn't wanted her to kn
ow where they lived but she's a
lready been inside the house. (
he left his keys behind one day
). she read their letters to ea
ch other from the melbourne & c
oober pedy periods: when maggie
told him not to trust her, that
she was an excellent actress, &
maggie thought she herself was
pregnant & wrote to say at leas
t the new baby would be a love
child born of love & laughter,
unlike claire

she'd read a stack of shop card
s from maggie to edouard for di
fferent occasions & went off at
claire in front of edouard for
buying one for her friend's bir
thday: 'you should make one up
yourself. what kind of friend
are you, if you can't think of
something to say yourself?' she
says edouard blanched

she says she drops in on edouar
d for coffee when passing with
the letter-box leaflets & he's
at home/maggie's working. one d
ay she returned down the other
side of the st. to see him pick
ing up her cigarette butts off
the ground fronting the veranda
h where she'd thrown them

she says she feels anger toward
s maggie, enough to be the wind
, though she doesn't know wheth
er she could ever live with edo
uard again even if he finally m
ade up his mind that way

*can you hear me in there? put your weapons down and come
to the hole. just come out where you see the light. go down on the floor
and crawl out the door where you came in. it's not going to get any
better. put your weapons down and come out the hole in the door
where you see the light*

all pink towelling shorts
she guides/pushes the lawnmower
over the lawn

she tries to give the impression
everything's casual
as she shaves the lawn into iron filings

that the flowers and shrubs haven't rusted
from the humidity of her body

that the grass filings haven't been magnetised
to follow the pattern of her footsteps

she tries to make her lips look like steel
she's swept up her hair
in an attempt to look unnatural like a steel-wool tree
to avoid attention

but us men hang around like dogs
can sense the heat

one frantically sweeps down the cement perimeter
frothing his house like a neurotic on speed

i walk past on the road
oblivious to a car crawling up my backside
my eyes surreptitiously stroking her like iron
into a magnetic shout
am nearly run over

we can feel her mowing our skin down
slicing off our body hairs with her mouth and fingers
like you'd slice off a forest of butter

our hearts are full of petrol fumes
and heavy breathing drowns out outersuburbia with its racket
as she guides us/pushes us
our metal-hardness a vibration
through her lawn

she can switch us on
anytime/and does

*i had, however, miscalculated the distance, and although he
made a desperate effort to clear the bush he came down crushingly on*

the shadows, some of whom must have been seriously injured and
probably killed, as i heard deep groans and hideous yells, which redou-
bled the fright of my already unmanageable charger, and i did not
succeed in pulling him up for some time afterwards

there is a brick i know of with glass walls

& inside this brick
there is a yellow machine
which scurries around
backwards & forwards
like a tadpole inside a glass jar

& the driver of this machine
is a glass helmet
attached to a glass air-hose attached
to a glass mouth

& fronting this machine
is a bucket lined with teeth

& inside this bucket
there is a brick faced with skin
& full of air
& space
to stretch out in

& this brick is a dumping ground
for bashings & smashings

& travellings
backwards & forwards
side to side
like a tadpole trapped inside a glass jar
in a bucket
inside a glass brick
inside

& we are inside
beside ourselves inside a brick i know of
with glass walls

        & inside this brick
        there is a machine that

go down on the floor. if you can hear me, go down on the floor and
come to the back door. go down on your hands and knees and crawl
along and put your head through the hole you put in the back door

i come across 'pania'
in the library among the bound journals
& ask her name/she's studying philosophy/
is back from sydney for a few years/lesley really/
given her 'name' in king's cross/
maori for 'girl of the sea'/
chris barnett/ larry buttrose & len linden in sydney apparently
with an act concerning adelaide friends & incestuousness/
'poetry is supposed to be fantasy' she says

richard in the refec eating/
his usual torn out crossword in front of him
& talking of summers at the general motors factory/
of lying on the paper to keep off the grease lunchtime/
being prodded & asked if he's o.k./'yes, i'm alright'/
the walls hosed down to try & cool it off/
his arrangement of metal in jigs for welding
into place

        anne in her red dress
        climbing the steps ahead of me/
        my feeling like patting her buttocks
        pressing thru/don't/
        she wondering if she'd see 'this guy'/me/
        fate?/
        she's back from sydney/
        from manipulating her words in interviews/
        not certain whether she'll be here
        or in london/not telling them that/
        they wouldn't be interested
        if she's going straight back/

trying for a holiday after the interviews
around the circular quay/'the rocks'/the opera house/
sick & tired of the lack of money/the grind of acting/
the need to reaffirm every day/
the determination you need to be successful/
we're waiting for a bus by the war memorial/
the memorial of the dead/
& as it arrives & turns the corner
i say i'm late for my film/i'll have to ring her/
her red dress/dracula red-black lips/
she asks whether i have the money to move to the city

upon looking about, i found i was considerably in advance of my
party, and retraced my steps a couple of miles or so, and met several
troopers with a number of captive shadows, and among them were
the shadows i had missed

black inside
(the outside
 ripe with
 colour)
a parrot
is heaped
against an apple

deadness
the aesthetic
causes me to
stumble

come on out. come out through that
back door. (BANG!) i know you have a rag over your face but i can
put more gas in there to take that rag away. go down on your hands
and knees and come out that hole. if you don't i'll put more gas in
there. put them weapons down. i know it must be hurting now. put
your weapon down. come on out. that's the only way you're going to
come out. you're in a no win situation. i can put more gas in there than

you've got already. come on, put your weapon down. come on, put
your weapon down

    the cinema.

                black & white people in the sts.
                the traffic noise of unseen traffic a constant roar
                as they face it/sitting on a fence/
                to sell their bodies or not like flowers/
                that is the question/to hawk themselves

                talking at each other without looking at each other
                mini-skirts/thin black ties
                a foreign worker is bashed & kicked on the ground/
                to return to greece is the answer
                bang-bang/boom-boom

    interval/

                a book on meditation/
                doug's woman/a coffee shop table/
                another table & chas

                doug wants to direct himself/
                he's tired out with working/
                marilyn monroe is watching us

                & that woman i wrote a letter to
                is below in a scarlet jumper & lipstick/
                white face like a clown's/'pale & wan'

                the consistent-constant dying (into death)

    talking outside
    & that woman in the red jumper talking to friends of hers
    who move out to look at me/a smile on their faces
    hers blank/mine slight
    & a glance at her back/her thin jeaned hips
    as they walk away

2 negroes from africa
arm in arm with a blonde in a mini-dress/red/
their loud conversation/words unintelligible
& a glance at their backs
as they walk away

*the result of that day's proceedings was the
capture by the land and boat party of sixty-five shadows. without
exception, they all wore articles of European clothing, belonging to the
murdered people, more or less stained with blood*

i pick the scabs
off my brain
– her words dribbling thru
  dried up

i'm on the dole
refuse to work 9–5
don't own a house
have never owned a car
have never been overseas
won't marry or have kids
hate the queen and the liberal party
hate god and he hates me

so my mother hates me
because she loves everything
i don't won't stand up for.
i hate her in turn, just to be fair

to me
she's a conquistador
melting down the artwork of my gold and culture
into characterless gold bars
for shipping back sanctified
to her country of relatives
money money money

to her
i'm a savage who
sacrifices and eats human flesh
and can't fight back
because i don't have the technology
of moral superiority,
a colour t.v. and mix-master.
i run around naked
in front of the neighbours of her mind

she's the catholic priests
burning all the mayan literature,
cutting a civilisation's wrist with fire
and owning the only ambulance in town

i'm satan sinner
and that wine that remains wine,
refuses to twist to blood
when she tackles it with transubstantiation
in the communion service
on sundays

she's hitler
and i'm the book at the burning of the books

i'm lenin in the bed
and better to be dead
than house a red in the bed

i'm ned kelly,
the imaginary copkiller,
she's the troopers
turned into the cops and asio of outersuburbia,
the brick veneers
with their vegetable lawns,
words and fantasies kept in place, well mowed.
lawns aren't grass,
they're god's benediction and hallelujah
on the protestant do's and don'ts
of australia, do take/don't give;
NO HORSES ALLOWED on the lawn
and at the dinner table

we talk to each other through
the medium of the t.v. set,
we're the characters in the soap opera
called mothers and sons,
we speak to each other
with cathode tube dialogue
and while asleep
we dream adverts
between the action

i dream of a revolution
and her execution.
while her head rolls, i knit.
i dream up a siberia
and a gulag of camps from our perma-frost,
one for each day of our year:
we take it in turns playing prisoner and guard

we must stop living with each other
before we try switching off each other's t.v. programme
permanently

      (BANG!) i told you, this is not going to improve. take the
board away from the door. move the board away (i'm watching you),
and come out. there's plenty more where that came from and it's not
going to get any better

my face covered with the sleep of stubble
from the night before 24 hrs later almost
as my eyes lie amongst the severed fish heads
their staring black eyes their heavy brooding grey
foreheads of glazed abstraction among the torn
backbones of supple pink flesh sagging
over the red white and black the heap of blood
the glutinous gut seeping into the ads.
on the back of the paper the classified CHEAP/
URGENT SALES columns of print and white pauses
like breaths my skin a rough rubble my eyes

raw scales wanting to be sick all over the paper
on the kitchen table as everything waits for my face
to make a decision about disposal the knife is stuck
to the paper with dry clotted blood the black
handle the steak of my face among the eyes of the fish
as they hesitate like lesions among the ads.
that have been sold to the highest bidder
for a dollar-eighty a kilo some distance from
the sea that now swims in my blood part of them swims
through my face my eyes are the savage crows
that read shadows into silence the white spaces
between words where there's no room to breathe
before the next word gets you and turns you back
on your own eyes that just hang there dumb

in the first hole, the shadow of a man with skull fractured. in the second hole the shadow of a boy of from twelve to fourteen years of age, the skull fractured over the right eye. in the third hole the upper part of the shadow of a man of a large size, the fracture very extensive. in the fourth hole the shadow of the skull of a woman, over the left eye a fracture. having made a very minute examination, we returned the shadows to the several holes from whence they were taken, and carefully covered them

'. . . . . the milk looks real clear.' 'oh well, we may as well dong it now, catherine.' 'i'll see ya, i don't know when.' 'oh, i'll see ya later on.' '. . . . . no, i'm not coming over. i might go to *strath* . . . .' 'what's its name? has it got a name yet?' 'fritz, that's what he'll turn into. bull calves aren't wanted.' the mother is licking it, he's trying to stand, still wet. there's after-birth, strings of it still on his coat, plus bran flecks and wood shavings. he bends a front white leg. the mother is up, some clear fluid from a bottle being fed into her neck via a tube. she bends her head back to lick the calf, 2 guys holding her. the calf, legs folded, makes a short struggle to stand, relapses continually, bends its head forward, strains. 'i think he's trying to get up.' the calf leans its head around and back as the mother licks its shoulder. the young farmer is hand-milking the cow into a yellow plastic bucket, thin jets of milky white. she's brown and white, an illawarra, he's black and white. she's licking the after-birth off his left shoulder. there's still a mass of white flecks on his body from where he lay. 'you going to *the creek* tonight?' 'no.' 'she's been treated with antibiotics, so . . . .' 'she just lost all her belly there.' he's gradually gaining strength, props partly up, falls back, she's still licking, his head now. a white mark on his forehead. 'that is so cute,' her brown tongue licking. 'i was going home in 10 mins.' laughter. 'stand up, little cow,' a young girl pleads. the sound of raspy licking. a death. a birth. while all this is going on i'm thinking of marianne's mother who died a short time ago. 'how long does it take before he stands up?' 'look! look! look! look!' as he almost does, his back still weak and disorganised. she's encouraging him by licking at his face and he's struggling to get away. 'it looks just like mum.' 'that's good timing, just on the last day . . . .' 'she's already missed the last ride. she has to go to *mount gambier*.' she looks up occasionally but then returns to the business of lick, lick, licking. 'a big bull, is it?' 'yeah.' 'here we go . . . . oh!,' as it pitches forward on its head. '. . . . . that was close . . . . unbelievable.' 'at least it wasn't twins, that was the last thing we . . . .' 'here we go . . . .' the back legs are still too weak to support it and he pitches forward again, kicking his mother's snout with a leg. she's maintaining the tonguing, shavings now around its mouth and nose. he's almost up, then not, the mother lowing and the calf making its first noise. again. one of the guys brings a layer of fresh baled hay he pulls apart and places under her head. she licks the calf, starts eating. '. . . . . almost!' 'oh yes, the legs are there, back legs are there . . . . won't be long now, just those front legs, has to straighten out its front legs . . . . amazing . . . .' 'jelly-legs.' a thread of umbilical cord hangs from its belly. 'not much meat on it.' 'it's exhausted just from doing that.' rain on the corrugated iron roof. there's a gap between them now and the 2 guys are pulling the name placards down from the wall. 'oh right, it's got an audience here!' it's expressing itself more loudly now, wants to be nearer her, though she's eating hay. its ears waggle as it quietly bawls. it's a dark brown, not black, just its wetness making it appear blacker. trying again, head down, propping like a triangle, back legs up. 'your attention, please, if ken follet is in the pavilion, could you come to the office, please,' coming over the intercom. the triangle of it moves forward as it shakes. 'nearly there.' 'nearly had it.' it's back on its side again. 'nature's cruel, if they don't get up.' 'come on, then.' the mother swings her head around. 'come on .... no, that's a bit hard. do you want to wait and see?' 'i want to wait and see.' one front leg out, straining. 'one more, mate, one more.' the guy tries to push it closer to the mother but can't move it. '.................. she died calving.' 'what's the time?' '5.30.' 'you want to go and see that fashion parade, don't you?' the cow swings her head around again, leaning forward, not quite reaching it. she patiently stands there as he struggles again. he's up. shaking, but up, straining forward, wobbling. the young farmer touches its neck and it imprints partly onto him. he waggles his fingers down its forehead. 'it just stood up ....', everybody's riveted. he falls onto a bag. 'time for a rest, eh mate?' he bawls, she moos. the guy lifts the calf up and carries it to the cow where it spends considerable time trying to find a teat to suckle on. it's finally getting warmer, nuzzling at the udder area nearer the teats, though it still doesn't have one. it's nuzzling up around her coat now, her belly, further away, now back the other way, the guy trying to guide its mouth. it finally finds one but the cow moves and it loses it. a thin stumpy tail, white-tipped. it wobbles around. the mother is licking it again and it continues to wobble around, walks under the cow and out this side, walks around her head and back in the teat direction. she chews hay. he's back under her neck, straw tickling his head. that red 'straw' hanging from his belly

'any similarity to persons living and dead
 is purely coincidental'
                    (read with a lisp)

the race is on to be the first,
to make the mcGOONess book of records.
it's called defrosting the royal baby,
in politer circles,
this getting in before anyone else does
and 'when will the royal family

          release a press release
          through *the mcGOONess book of records*
          of the first fucking?'
no doubt will become the paramount catch-cry
behind our nation's great push forward
into the future

the nanny would have to be odds on
in betting circles
to have first option,
being so close,
but you might be able to get to the baby
through the nanny.
interesting to know how he feels later,
knowing some strange woman
has been fiddling around with his prick
in the bath
for years

his mother could also have designs

i wonder what the ripples would be
if she eloped with her son,
had a right royal relationship.
would it be the first case of incest
in the royal family?
could the queen hush it up?

his relationship with his father on the polo field
could develop into a mauling situation
in years to come:
watch *the women's weekly*
for stories of 'accidental' bruises
incurred.
it makes his father dangerous,
of course,
and he could well be fucked up by his father
as well as the system

(and watch the bodyguards)

he might be male
but there's more than one hole
that's serviceable,
and babies are great at sucking:
he couldn't bite it off
like some woman once did in brazil
to her lover

and fucking the royal baby
could be the ultimate terrorist act.
i could find myself out in the royal garden
behind a long line of
trench-coat wearing irish accents.
better get in quick:
no need to stick around –
short, sharp and shiny will do

then again,
if everyone's too prurient,
i'll settle for being the first one
to vomit over the little bastard
– true aussie conceptual art
   in the vein of *bazza mckenzie*
   and *stork*
he can lick it up
for baby food

> *i started with my party, and after beating about the bush for
shadows in every direction, we found, rammed into an animal hole, the
bodies of two men and one woman, which we afterwards buried as
decently as we could. their skulls were fearfully battered in. near the
woman was a large, heavy family Bible, which the poor creature must
have carried for days after the wreck*

> running for the bus
> stopped at my regular stop
> running for the next stop

slicing an eye like a mushroom
chopping an eye on a chopping board
like chopping parsely
one hand down hard on the end of the blade
one swivelling quickly/in stabbing
the handle down hard & breathless
with a hard (resisting) (unresisting) excitement to its edge

the audience on the edge of its seat

a guy running for the bus
as it starts to move
shouts out 'hey'.
i shout out 'there's a guy coming'/
the bus continues.
the driver is oblivious/
maybe i didn't cry out loud enough
or he ignored me on purpose/
i'm unsettled/
nobody else in the bus said anything/
he's left behind us
    no doubt swearing blue murder

crumpled up like paper/a blood & bone ball
the sheep nest amongst the grass
& eat their nests
as they grow

a body on a stretcher/oxygen mask/white tight sheets/
an ambulance/
cops in blue talking to a woman in bright purple/
an all-swathing dress/
the white lined skin of her face/auburn hair
mouth talking/opening & closing silently
as if answering questions/
details of the accident perhaps/
there's a black bike standing nearby on the concrete

she looks like helen in that mauve jumper
anchored to her skin
words & pictures/headlines & bylines

sliding up & down her skin below the wool
& as i turn to glance back
i notice a cop's face/his hat(e) & uniform/
sitting behind me
  also glancing back/
      his movements are shadowing mine

'democracy is applauding'
                graffiti on a shop wall

(BANG!) put your weapon down and come out. come out the same
way you went in. move that piece of wood out. put the weapon down.
get down and come out with your hands up. that gas can be quite
harmful. get down, remove the piece of wood from the door and come
out

  it's my first swallow for the summer
  its black flight mowing the grass
  swerving the colour from green to yellow
  and swallowing the tail of winter

  i look for its breast-flash
  a hint of a monroe kiss
  from days when lips left their suicidal mark
  and every kiss was an endpoint in itself

  this flight through an eye, in one corner
  and out the other, is a red tear
  the air torn open
  to let us both jump through the hoop

              lorikeets
              with vermilion bands and beak
              green-iris camouflaging
              are acrobats
              swinging on trapezes of green gum leaves
              tips

                    they carry their very own safety net
                    their green-yellow tail feathers
                    which spray out like palm fronds
                    parachuting

galahs
chemical mixtures of fire and water
exploding christs of fire and rain
scissors
a war of suspended animation of colour
tearing
clashing
bruising into halves
heartbeats perching pulsing
ruffled energies straining out their splattering echoes
of rain collapsing on hot ash

they are playground clowns
gymnasts representing only themselves

and stacked in trees
like cans in a supermarket
they play out their courtship games
sidling up
sidling down
crests cocked and ready to shoot

at another spot in the same neighbourhood, in shelters of the shadows,
we found newspapers, receipted bills in the name of the captain of the
wreck, a number of letters, a book, part of the log, and the torn leaves
of a Bible

cinema.
            the acting false. brad davis

            brother fucking/in love with/brother

the fight ritualised/the stylised talking
to screen & camera/talking to air

an interview
                    cigarette waving around
about chasing fame in america/his desire
                    to live in new york

        working with stars now instead of unknowns

        'just be brilliant'/to jeanne moreau
        as she steps out of a car to start work

        she walks up twisted steps to a studio
        & disappears thru a door

*alright, i can hear you in there, i can hear you laughing. i can
hear your comment. it's a matter of who has the last laugh. come on
out. you're not going to come out any other way. it's better that you
come out yourself than we have to come in and get you*

        my thoughts dogpaddle
                    spin me
                    like wheels
                    fast or slow
        depending on the
                    hand's press

        blonde hair cascading
                    a waterfall falling
                    lying on the
        sand sanding by the water's edge
        that extensive pool
        tan fine-tuning under the sun
        as it green-water lies –
        stretched out   absorbing reflections

        there's a violence-radiation
        of the physical that
        burns the sun to dark

dancing
acceleration that kills dying
a green-hair ciao

my mouth open
i lie below your fall
your hair rushes down my throat
spreads out
to heart and lung
a brain
a vein
below my skin/injections

you slake me
    make me

i swim your surface
with a lazy breast stroke

*before daybreak the following morning we were
again on horseback, and recommenced scouring the sand-hills and
valleys, and we descried a couple of shadows who wore European
clothing, which they threw away the better to escape us by swimming*

the bus ride/
a guy with long blonde hair to a woman
can i sit there?   don't you trust me?
shakes her head   he shuffles the word 'paranoia'

the lights like pinpricks through a sheet of black paper/
cut off by a hill/a depression

    returning home with my form
                still not taken in

*   come out. put the weapon down on the floor and
come out into the open air. come on out. put your weapon on the
ground inside the shop and come on out. so, come on out. this is not
going to resolve itself while you are standing in there. put your weapon*

83

down. this is not going to help you by staying in there. this is not going to help you or anyone else

when i come out into the kitchen
late at night
and switch on the light
i see them making a run for it
across the sink
among the dishes
across the breadboard
among the crumbs
and down the tea-chest

i hear them dropping their paper bags
and heading for dark holes
at the end of skirting boards

i hack down hard with boots or shoes

and sometimes manage one or two
easing and oozing them out their wings
and back
and they always seem to die hard

i baygon a kiss over the room

and come out later
to find them sprinkled over the floor
of the kitchen and bathroom and toilet
in love-knots

the odd one twisting and spinning slowly
around its back
and back on itself
as it fights its insides slow and hard
kicking out at the air with legs and feelers
and wondering at the shadow
inside of it

and it's then that i always think of cornflakes
that move

as the shadows had already gained some distance into the lake, and it was evident they would escape, the major ordered two of the police to fire. the first shot at them evidently told, by the sound of the thud which followed

the ash trees struggle
to reflect the sky in their own image
by drawing it down into the water
with them,
drowning it
by holding it under

the river moves through winter
carrying the dead semen
of autumn

nobody
wants to touch the water
for real:
they just move with memories
from the time
their ex left that cold patch
beneath the sheets
and in their mind
and try to keep themselves
together
for some new spring

the bars i visit
are like winter rivers
and we line the edge,
dropping our thoughts
into the ice-filled booze,
feeling it rush away
down our throat
to some far away sea

the urinal is overflowing
with everybody's
used up and discarded thoughts

we flick some drops
over each other's
shoes

       put your weapon down and come out. come out through
the door. put your hands down and come out through the door. put
your weapon down and come out. come through the doorway. i want
to talk to you

she shacked up with him for his quiet strengths
his different way of looking at things
and they enjoyed their first enthusiams of the deep north together

and then he started to build his dam on contract labour
with the D-10 dozer the macho dozer
the kudos proportional to the size of the machine
while she relaxed her contraception/he agreed
he liked the idea/she removed her IUD
became pregnant/started building herself her own dam

and he would travel to work from the caravan park by the highway
at 7 in the morning
returning 5.30 in the afternoon
while she stayed home working

and he sitting all day on the screaming dozer pushing
dirt and dust and shit uphill into a wall/the tracks
wincing savagely like ballerinas in boots as they screwed round
on themselves to try another direction/more leverage/push push
macho man/tiring hot and thirsty work/for men only
no room for boys and women

visiting the pub on the coast/drunk all weekend
drinking at the pub with his workmates until they dropped
or vomited/raced off each other's wives and girlfriends
telling his workmates he'd have to take the baby camping when it came
drinking more/always more cans to empty/small dams in the hands

the talk about how to fix the girlfriend who'd ripped a thousand dollars
worth of dope off one of them/give her herpes
cut her arms off/etc and etc

changing his character and picking fights
shouting abuse out of speeding boozing cars
threatening to shove guys' teeth down their throats
and relying on his build to be the best

she not drinking because of the baby inside her
he applauding the fact while sober but being the last to leave the party
trying to outdrink everyone else/telling her to go on home alone
if she wanted to go

the photo of the baby resting on her stomach a day out of hospital
she surprised at how big she was/wondering how she'd carried her around
inside the chaos/the tears/the arguments

the continuously crying baby/the continually crying music/racket
from downstairs in the house shared with other males and males
and even more males stretching out to her horizon
and he without the gutz to tell them to turn it off or down

and plenty of photos and dirty nappies/drinking and noise and drinking
and she cleaning up his vomit with an afterwards resignation
and attempted understanding she now regrets/he saying
he'd pull himself together soon

and the dam wall higher/the machine inside her whining away
grinding away at her winning margin until she couldn't stand it any longer
and packed herself together like a lunch for the south
he accusing her of pissing off on him
as he backed the dozer out of the hole in the wall of her body
its tracks backing and bucking in air/he freefalling out
with his machine a metal parachute refusing to open

the hole in her vacated heart a mess of tracks left lying around
like dirty washing on the bedroom floor
tracks impregnated in the air like a mural of chaos
interrupted sex/a pattern of birth
the imprint of feet and knees and punching hands sculptured
on her bag of skin

the dozer lying at her feet/a toy turtle on its back
its metal driver slumped in its seat

she treading on it as she walked away
spinning her shoes/doing a wheely

while down south she stuffs and refills the hole with extra time
and the separation/patches her skin with her friends and the baby

and realises she has given birth to a baby that's just another bulldozer

but in crossing a valley open to their view, the shadows evidently caught sight of us, and guessed our object, and consequently altered their course in the direction of an island, about a mile and a half from the shore. i quickly rode down to the margin of the water

michael & eating & talk
about living at perrin's boarding house/hostel
run by a woman who takes no nonsense/
oldish guys who keep to themselves/
one guy going on a drinking spree
& not paying for 8 days/leaving in the morning
& back at night/she having no key & at his door
knocking & shouting/'i've known you for some time'/
her male friend climbing in through the ceiling
& shouting back/'he's drinking & lying on the bed,
the fucker'/the health inspector arriving another time
& mike quick to throw his mess together under the bed/
she standing at the door & smiling as the inspector
walks in/an aboriginal who sneaks in his mates/
visitors to be out by 10/corridors & rooms
that stretch right back/100s/$30/wk./no meals/
a communal kitchen hardly anyone uses/
no bond or lease or receipts

it's not going to do you any good by staying in there. now come on. you can do your fingers trick later. you must be a 'port' supporter. i can see your black and white beanie. you haven't done anything wrong now other than you shouldn't have been in there in the first place but that's nothing that can't be resolved

the schoolgirl floats in the horse's belly

i cling to the shadows
that stick to moist hands

as her dress follows the religion
of her body

she observes the jumps
thru the horse's eyes

the churned ground leaps up
to meet her
as she takes it easy/in her stride
lands in my mouth

my hands padlocked away
i kiss her bubbles of thought
from my comicbook fantasies
and wait for the horse to take me in hand

her dress rides up her body
as the horse floats over the jump
and parachutes to earth
silk legs and tapering fingernails

caught short of action
i slink off back to sideshow alley
where games are games
horses are tin or plastic or ceramic
and schoolgirls remain at the other end
of telephones

*being a strong swimmer in those days i gained rapidly upon
the shadows and soon reached the island myself. i followed the tracks
of the shadows, which were marked by blood, and discovered them
behind a thicket. one was lying down, supported by the other, and as i
approached they commenced a series of lamentations and bewailings,
repeating dolefully the words: 'very good white fellow'*

so this is how you build an amniotic sac
these days

buy a farm
subdivide
build roads for access
dig trenches for water & sewerage pipes
flatten a piece of ground
cement foundations in
construct a wood-white skeleton/a web
brick in walls for facing the gaps
tile
glass
connect the umbilical cord of
electrical wiring sewerage pipes & mortgage
& inside this controlled environment place
the happy couple
who monitor their history & growth
turn-ons/turn-offs
yes/no's
with the flick of a switch
up & down
down & up
just like sex
where they try for a regulation 2
a dick & jane or anne & peter
& a regulation life
of t.v./lounge suite/new used car/occasional visits
to barbecues & votes & wondering why & how

but
there's a stage
when everyone has to leave the sac or drown
learn
to take their own 2 chances
stand on their own 2 feet
run & laugh outside the silence of their beginnings
leave the water for the beach

& it's high time tide for us

put your hands down on the floor and creep out the hole now. put your
gun down, put your hands on the floor and come out the hole now. all
this is not going to help you at all. all that means is we'll have to put
more gas in. you have to come out yourself

        train. priority seats for aged
            or disabled persons

```
┌─────────────────────────────┐
│         Land                │
│   General Industrial        │
│                             │
│      FOR SALE               │
└─────────────────────────────┘
```

a white sign with red lettering amongst the iron sheds
        we're swaying through

heads enter the subterranean world beneath the gravel/
the walkways heading down/& a girl with a plait & freckles
            disappears
                down the steps
                    in a jagged movement/
                            a merino motion

    a speedboat leaves a white slice in the sea

an old man & old woman sit behind their sunglasses

        a young girl eats a chocolate bar/
    she pokes it towards her mouth & the skin of paper crackles/
        her closed mouth chews & moves its load around/
            she's absorbed

        i'm taking my form in. the window reveals the sea
                    & the large W pinned to a tower/
                the chainstore church

a woman with a pram sits
as if hypnotised by a small child ahead of her on her mother's lap
bows & plaits above her ears
& eyes out the window on the bank & its overwhelming height
which threatens to drown her in dirt.
the woman blots her up/

her idea of the picture perfect child perhaps/
her looks & energy/alert eyes
& her own child/the same age
sits on her lap & takes her in as well/
not nearly as pretty though
& she tiredly lays her head against her mother
as if already resigned

there's a pregnant woman further on in dazzling colours
& poles & lines & branches swirl past in a startle of parallels

the shadows were bleeding profusely, and,
naturally, thinking they must soon die from the effects, i left them and
returned to the shore

i am a white bone of flower inside my body
which is a web which rings like a white bell

i have forgotten my name

my eyes are full of sold
and laughter is a scratchmark across the scrawl of my skin
like sex on a tattooed brain

i have to flex myself to laugh

i am a comic comicbook hero of the gothic
and carry around a scalding potato beneath my tongue
like a blonde tear

i suck on wounds these days
that are my exhaustion and my leaving

i am on the long way to nowhere but here
and say hullo to the choking choke of my breathing

i am the mud of my heart
which slips through my fingers as i lick it

i am out of love with my lack of power
and there is no transfusion
but the confusion of my laughter with gravel
which drops through the holes in my tongue

i am the torn sounds of an athlete

i am the sounds of a white bell
which is the paralysing flower of the bone in my eye

i am the cold breath of my eyes. that breathe what i eat

i am at the beginning of the end of my own beginning

i have outgrown my stem which was green

and once again i am being forced to approach it all
from the sideways angle. instead of upfront

*in the shop. we're still here. we're waiting. put the guns down
and come out. if not, just talk to me. what's your name? tell me what your
name is*

we were both hungry with drunk

                    she was so drunk i had to continually
hold her hand so she could stand

                    i was so drunk i couldn't pull myself together
to stand up inside her even with a helping hand

  the trouble was the thing we were both after was sober
and scuttering around the other side of the glass/
  outside the aquarium

she'd even knocked over a glass of wine
which i didn't quite lap up off the carpet

the only thing that seemed to be able to stand in the room
was the erection on a black new guinea mask/cowries for eyes
and guillotine lips/and even that needed to lean against the wall
for support

we were inside her bedroom trying to dry ourselves off
on the inside
by towelling ourselves down with soft words

like how she had been in love
how she used to play out her shy-games with him
how he'd rung her in sydney to her surprise/he trusted her/
that was her commitment to him
and then back here his girlfriend blowing his brains out
and then her own
leaving her scrambling with the ifs and buts and misdirections
and outcomes

at that stage i felt like i'd been caught inside a tropical rainstorm
inside a fish pulled inside out like a wet glove to dry/
a downpour inside outside i was dry as a bone

she'd really managed to rain on me before i'd put up my umbrella

my tongue was soaked through with her matted words/a jungle of rain
and pain

    by morning she'd wrapped herself up in a dark-blue sheet/
    her body bag/and as i left i buried her inside her underwater room/
    the burial of a body all at sea

    and relieved the pressure walled up inside myself
    by pissing in the park outside
    while a black swallow flew rings around me

        during the day the captive shadows made it known that
one of the murderers of the crew of the wreck was on the mainland
opposite our camp, and could be secured. subsequently two of them,
with our interpreter, were permitted to go over and bring him to us,
which they did in the afternoon. they pointed out one of their number
also as being the murderer of a whaler. both these shadows, voluntarily
given up by the others, were powerfully made, and stood nearly six feet
high, with countenances the most ferocious and demon-like i ever
beheld

      eating peter & kirsten
        & the naïveté of che guevara fighting a revolution
        in a strange land/no cushy job/but the romantic
        revolutionary/the byron losing control of reality

& success to fill in a hole with bullets
after the blood has flown out the gap
of idealism brought up short/a diarrhoea
of the heart & will/
            the nicaraguans fighting/
the perfection in question marks of cuba/
the 6 teachers holding off the bay of pigs
invasion & the name Fidel written in blood on
the wall as the last one dies/applause
for the worker-soldier heroes returning to the factory
floors of cuba from the african factories of blood
& bath & fist thrown bullets/no vietnam yet/
the socialist from america talking/dreaming
about the new age

jean & her return from sydney/hitching/
the cold indifference of canberra/
being picked up at balranald by a guy
who talked about his asian trip where he was treated
like a king/shouting her meals

she plays a bat in the zoo for a thousand school-kids
who throw peanuts/she plays a rabbit/a human
with rabbit thoughts

in the shop. put your gun down and come to the door and come out. you're not in serious trouble. come out and talk

we sit in her vw on hindley st. and outside my place

she's trying to put up a cold front and shut me out
and i'm trying to give her the hots

we make our moves simultaneously

she feels financially emotionally sexually secure, or so she claims,
with her present lover

though he's 16 yrs older and she wants to have kids at some stage,
with a career, and she doesn't know about him

and she feels infatuations for other guys at times
which i'm trying to play on and use for my own benefit

as i progress from a hand on her leg to a goodbye kiss forever
that extends to my tongue in her mouth hand on her buttocks
among the awkwardness of the vw front seat
behind the steering wheel

and it's a st. where cops regularly patrol,
so it's one eye open

with cars using the spaces in front and behind us like musical chairs

and couples leaving the pizza parlour across the road
and using us as an aphrodisiac

as her hair grows stringier and stringier soggier and soggier
with the saliva and heat

and her telling me to calm down
and 'get a job' (to change my way of life)
    'buy a house' (i can't keep on sharing forever)
    'take up jogging' (because i have the build and need to run off
                some energy)
    'find a woman' (to also release some energy) 'soon'
and keep my hair short (as it is, because it suits me)

and i tell her i have a woman/her and i love her
and i mean a little of it but not much
though i do find her erotically attractive so i have to go overboard
to keep her attention and i realise she probably realises that
but i'm appealing to her romanticism and vanity
and dissatisfaction with her present lover and fantasies about the future

though she doesn't believe i could sacrifice myself for anyone
so i have to say i could for her/i'd chop off a leg if necessary
and the thought repulses me but when you're hot you're hot

and i've undone her blouse by now by pulling apart the grey knot at the ▪
with my teeth
and her buttons with my left hand
and have my hand on her bra and can only feel her left nipple below it
           (which is rather off-putting)

with her claiming that her breasts are large (though they don't seem so to me)
and us touching each other's face up (quietly) with our lips and fingers
                    (there are bursts of energy/bursts of quiet)

and the taxi guys opposite in the depot with some sort of drive-in show

and just then a sound as if something's hit the car
so we spring apart and look innocent and look around
but there's nobody about
(and it's only later i find out that the people i share with
 are up on the balcony watching and killing themselves laughing
 because one of them's thrown the something
 that has hit the car)

but anyway the two of us get back together again

and i unlock the button of her jeans and zip
and have my hand on the top of her pubic hair
        (though she won't allow me further)
and our kisses are hotter in temperature and her lips seem softer
and there's more heavy breathing and i figure i might be winning

when a cop car pulls up in the st. in front of us/lights out
and i have to pull back out of being on top of her
in the vw front seat behind the driving wheel

and they're just sitting there and we're just sitting there
and they must have stopped because of us and nobody is making a move
and she says they can defect her (car i mean)

so i cajole her into driving around the back
and she does a u-ee and we end up driving in a circuitous route
and park-stall amongst the cars out back of my place

where the kissing starts all over again and someone drives in off the st.
wanting to park so she has to park in a space (properly)

where the kissing continues with more interruptions of more cars coming along
and more parking and more mobs disappearing into the building

and her zip's open again
(and she still won't allow my hand far down the front)
so i concentrate on her bare buttocks below her jeans and panties

and her hands are applying more pressure on me now
and we're still behind the wheel her side

and she's forgotten or tossed out her resolutions
though she won't come in with me
and i wonder whether i can induce an orgasm in her by pressing her left buttock
                      (now there's a fantasy for you)
and one in me by pressing my penis in my pants on her left leg
                (and that's another one)

and there's lots of tongue kissing and heavy breathing and limited movement
between the steering wheel and the seat

and sweat

and she's looking more beat up
as she moves over to sit on top of me after negotiating the gear-stick

and i have my hands on her buttocks and my penis comes out
and i masturbate its hardness as she's sucking my ear
so that i come all over my clothes next to her cunt
which is protected still by the barrier of her jeans and panties

and she's blowing cool air all over the sweat on my face
and is pleased she's held out against me at the end

and everything's an anti-climax now as it always is after a climax
as the eroticism walks off/she drives off as usual/she's escaped again

after she's/we've stood around exercising our joints for a while
and talked quietly about small things

           to insure the security of all the captive shadows for th
night, we made them sit in a ring and pinioned their arms with tether-rope
a large blazing fire was kept in the centre, so that the sentries could at one
see whether there was any disposition on the part of the shadows to make a
attempt at escape

     the skyscrapers in this unknown city
     reflect red seas in all their office windows
     & faces/they are our faces/seas we have seen

& the seas are ripples/seas
that reflect our graffiti of hunger/
the boats that sometimes float
are sinking under the weight of the certain words
we despair of

searching for money/slapping faces/
shooting your mistress when she's horny/
catching flies/collecting them/cooking
& eating them at a formal dinner party
like currants/the difficulty of using
a knife & fork/trying to resist the desire
to use a moistened finger to lift each individually
to your lips

laughter like dead flies/we open our mouth & expect
laughter to fly in/our hunger for laughter & satisfaction
is extreme/a revolutionary's addiction to action

> you have to applaud a woman
> for poisoning her husband, lover,
> father, children, friends, brother
> in order to maintain her independence/
> when it's the only way it's the only way/
> not to would be a cop out/
> i can hide the act away for future reference

*we know you came to the shop yesterday morning to buy a weapon. we
know you came back and stood outside the shop. it's no good shaking
your head. i can keep pumping gas in there all day and i know who'll
give up first*

> jeanie has given up the job
> of being katy the kangaroo
>
> kids no longer try to hop
> in her pouch,
> pull her ears off,
> (or her tail),

call out she's a big fat pig
and look with disbelief
through the dressing room door
when her head's being skun off

she no longer bluffs her way
into their open mouths like pouches

but she can go back
to being human again

while in the library
photos are displayed in glass cases
of south-east bushfire victims,
kangaroos
who've been given a fire shave
and burnt smooth like black eyeballs,
heads thrust through cyclone fences
and trying to graze, hungry for breath,
on the other side of death

their heads made it
but heads can't live alone

and it's far too late now for them
to be kangaroos again

'gentlemen, by virtue of the authority vested in me by his Excellency the gov
ernor, i declare, in the presence of Almighty God and of those assemble
around me, that i believe these two shadows who have been given over to us b
their own group, to be guilty of murder, and to merit death. this i declar
according to my conscience, so help me God'

the grey-white gums fight themselves upwards

it's been a long drawn-out winter
of little sun
to tan them
as they bathe in the blue sky
parked over their dirt beach

up the hillside
a butterfly breathes
while tea stirs an iron cup
and a blue table spreads out for miles
above their weight
in seconds

and as i walk
i hear the sounds of crickets
like underground raindrops
falling upwards
onto the soles of my shoes

the bus is blown down the freeway
as if a fag-end flicked
towards the city

that gull. a piece of paper
tossed into the air
above the museum

a piece of weather
under glass

o.k., so you've made a name for yourself. you've had your
hands on a gun. if you have a mental problem let me know and i'll see
if someone can come down and help you. if you want to talk to an
interpreter let me know what language you speak and i'll get someone
down to talk to you in your native tongue. are you german, polish,
yugoslav, greek? tell me and i'll get someone down to talk to you in
your native tongue, an interpreter, in 10 minutes

the black and white magpie crouches
its claws embedded in the branch

it spies on the ground
moving away from beneath it

it is a black and white crab
clutching onto a branch for comfort
way up off the ground
and kilometres from the sea

cushioned by green hills
and plenty of grass
sheep walk shadows like dogs

the branches are petrified tracks
along a beach
melted away by casual breathing

the black and white crab
anxiously guards the spaces between the branches
against their predators

those empty spaces
stranded by a previous tide

kilometres from the sea
the black and white crab perches in a shorn tree
and waits for the tide to scuttle back sideways
in the form of ice

the black and white crab
is a renascent idea in the head
of a black and white magpie
which waits to be disturbed

the major – 'bob, do you say these shadows have killed white men and
            ought to die?'
            'yes.'
            'charley, do you?'
            'yes.'
            'peter, do you?'
            'yes.'

she's my sister. i should touch her
with my tendrils of pain affection,
draw her into my kiss,
gnaw off pieces of love and experience,
devour, ingest and excrete
for my propulsion through this
overshadowed sea

but contact
has been lost

too long apart,
too few common connexions,
she exists outside them now
and her first child grows inside
the ballooning bubble of air and water,
a swimmer still tied to the shore,
not mine. theirs

i can visualise its tentacles developing,
growing under the fertilising umbrella
of her blood and bone,
irrigated by her dreaming

and when it finally breaks out and off
it will devour her,
leaving me nothing but the husked shell
of its own rejections
to mouth at,
like a stranded fish
too long out of water,
a swimmer too long
in water

her present has outswum our past,
left it behind
as a relic
on the sand
for surrealistic beachcombers like me
to pick up and finger,
then drop

you in the shop. go straight to the hole in the door and come out. leave the guns inside. leave the guns inside and come straight to the door. we've had enough. leave the guns in the shop and come straight through

bus.
      no, she said.
          no. his hands behind the seat/
no doubt groping her/she self-consciously
turning to see where i was/i was looking out the window
but the window couldn't help acting as a reflective surface/
whether she understood that
i don't know
but she was aware i was behind them
& that seemed to matter

train silhouettes side-on
they carry our eyes

                              (german monroe
the camera frisks light-poles   says)
     zip-zip

if i bent down close
to study my reflection in the rails
i could allow my head to be smashed
& not appear to be committing suicide

how can you face your indifference? (the suicide lover)

the laughter is artificial & ∴ brittle.
if i threw my laughter on the ground (asphalt)
it would break/like glass
it wouldn't bounce

the bus is a bus of ACTIVE WASTE SERVICES

looking up the corridor
you have all that space ahead of you/
you're no longer cramped

& that does make a difference.
distance & perspective are not the same

the cars are terrorised/
they run round with mufflers beneath their legs
like (dogs') tails

the two condemned shadows were handcuffed together, marched in
front under the special charge of two police troopers and myself; the
other shadows followed, escorted by the rest of the police

a sawn-off and thrown-away   thing
(a sawn) gum butt
  its roots
  twisted and curled
  like some disease
        and stubborn
awkward
smouldering with the suffocation
  of a broken off passion (thrusting)
            that thrust down
              (that has failed)
  it lies there now
  licensed
  a tethered dog of wood put down
    dissected
  a laboratory heart in a museum of air
    under glass/under wraps
  there is no room for giants now
      the taproot of children

there are no overpowering realities
  left among the fantasies
        in this sameness
          of sawn-up principles
only
    (the panic of the bitten)

once upon a time
it held wild eyes
in its wild palms
and the eyes breathed on the palms

now

leave the guns inside. we're not trying to hurt you. you can finish as
soon as you come out the shop. come on. come on now. put the gun
down

i force myself to (be an) animal
i realise i must force myself to realise
i'm an animal if i'm to survive (if i'm game to survive)
in this late late (20th
this latent condition of wash/wear/rubbing out/robbing
i crouch at the drinking hole
my legs & arms hunched
clear a space in the liquid's surface
push away the cigarette butts with hands/paws
my ears are all sound (ear)
my nostrils all smell (nostril)
my eyes all sight (eye)
the back of my neck
prickles with quick
blood & hair
walking edges
minus nets
my tension alert/with digesting my environment/cramps
in my stomach
from fear/the threat/the thing that creeps/
a coiled spring/a rush of blood/to pull me down/& out/
to acid my dreams
& bones/
i pull my face to the pool
& scoop away the debris for my reflection/the cigarette butts/
my tongue pulls out/pulls in the urine
from the urinal/my watering hole/i lap & slake my thirst

& the smell of burnt urine burns my heart
i hunch/my muscles quiver/my head darts round
i unstake myself
i quickly leave the spot/open
& another takes my place
a long line of me is waiting to take my place
in this time for animals only
in this late late (20th
& it's later than we think

with that look on my face of constant inbred surprise

*on arrival at the place of execution, which was about fifteen miles
from our camp, we halted; but as the whole strip of land is destitute of
trees of any size, one of us was despatched to the mainland to cut
down the tallest Shea Oaks he could find, with which to erect the
gallows. this, however, did not occupy much time*

as we approach we try to separate what is cloud
what is sea and what is land

we think of iron sheds.
there will be sheds everywhere

everything is uncertain.
from the distance everything blurs

there will be a dog near every shed.
perhaps

we hear the sound of iron scrape against the blur
and think of things gone sour from too much waiting

the island never stops
and in the end we blur together

*i assure you, you will not be hurt. you will not
be hurt, provided you leave the guns inside the shop. we will help you
when you come out. you will not be hurt*

& horses outrun us on rubber wheels
    their eyes cemented in oblivion

a whey-faced child says
        'horsey'   'horsey'
& a friend of its mother says
        'cow'   'cow'

we pass a tanker full of
    horses' legs
broken off at the joint
                (all of them broken at the knees)

from a far-enough distance
people are faceless
all they are are a blob of colour
your husband/wife/lover
could be making love to another
in front of your eyes (face)
& you wouldn't recognise them

            This vehicle
        is fitted with security
            devices

        NO ENTRY

        Passengers
        must not stand
        on front platform

        Priority seats
        for aged
        or disabled persons

        WAIT FOR LIGHT
THEN PUSH DOOR HANDLE TO OPEN

        STOP

PLEASE LEAVE BY CENTRE DOOR   (2 ways)

        SMOKING IS PROHIBITED
        IN THIS VEHICLE

Evaporative cooling system
operates more effectively
when some windows open

KEEP CLEAR OF DOORWAY
Passengers must not stand in stepwell

emergency exit

emergency exit –
Push window out

PLEASE DEPOSIT
used tickets
here

the rain stabs/nails/the windows
to the bus
water over eyes
the tail-lights of cars are shimmering red with emotion
the st. lights a yellow & out of control
                              (dissolving under pressure)

a breakdown that's no clown
deadpan not slapstick

i hop off the bus
& the rain increases its territory/
its juggernaut

*whilst the foregoing preparations were going on, the whole of the
shadows formed a semi-circle in front of the gallows. not a word or
whisper escaped their lips, and no attempt was made by the condemned
shadows to utter a word to the assembled group, but they stood per-
fectly dogged and resolute to the last*

last night i borrowed $4 from the food kitty to see *gilda*/
a black & white film of the 40s i hadn't seen for about 20 yrs
since a scrubbed-off adolescent watching sunday night t.v.

i remembered a black dress, a glove, a nightclub, a torch song,
& rita hayworth as the body

sex was a nervous perspiring after girls at school in those days
like the girl with no name & the purple check dress
that always seemed stained
& my history teacher who exiled me from the room for smiling at her
as if she was nefertiti
& marie burton with her cleopatra haircut/a real mod (yeah, yeah)

in those days i had calf eyes among school desks & words
& hands up air

presumably i know what sex is all about now/still intangibles
with no-one in bed beside me but memories that've grown spare tyres/
women & girls circulating in my washing machine of a mind
& pegged out to dry.
i wear them no closer than my skin

for sexual thrills i scrape off wet dreams like the one i had this morning
– a woman clad only in a top seducing the aisle as i yanked off
    under a desk

i'm a catastrophe in love

my room now consists of a desk & action on paper/marilyn monroe posters
& sunday night movies always in colour
& i live in a st. of nightclubs where the stars are transsexual
& the singer old & battered with fat & singing torch songs
that wouldn't set fire to moses' beard

& cars operate the st. all night like a drive-in nightclub for take-aways
looking for sexual hamburger/
while i'm still thinking of love. i'm still in love with me
& can't relax

you must leave the guns inside and not bring them with you. come out
the opening to the shop but leave the guns inside. come on now. open
the hole in the doorway. leave the guns inside

i am only an adult on paper

i am bound up inside a childhood
of book designs and illustrations

where figures crouch and breathe
breath is a machine heavier than air
and i fly through dangerous dreams

i am a matter of metal and skin
and figures that surround me

figures that crouch
and manipulate words

that carry guns full of words
that force me to fly me
through the black and white worlds
of their imagination

i believe them
i obey them

i also carry a gun full of words.
i pull it out
and whirl
and shoot
through the skin of my dreams
and hit me

i stagger and fall
through my own arms

i breathe out my last words
to myself.
i am the only one left
to hear me

i live in a world of plots
and counterplots
that have conspired against me

i have crashed to the ground
where only my bones walk away.
the rest of me burns
like paper

i am an english bushfire
called biggles

*when everything was reported ready, the two shadows were made to
stand on a box, expressly brought for that purpose. the nooses were
then passed over their heads, and the slipknots having been properly
adjusted, the box was suddenly withdrawn at a given signal, but unfor-
tunately the fall was not sufficient to cause the dislocation of the neck,
besides which the ropes stretched to such an extent, with the immense
weight of the shadows, that they remained simply suspended, their
toes touching the sand, and their eyes glaring upwards at the cross-
beam*

i'm a practical
man

but
for all my practicality
i can still hear
my god
mutter and scream
in the air
around
me

i throw him
a fish

*you will not be hurt. there is no need to be hurt. your eyes will be
hurting. your throat will be hurting. leave the guns inside – there is no
need for them – and come out. put your hands down on the floor and
come out the door*

the schoolgirl with the schoolgirl

you want a kid's ticket
i always wear a uniform
so the busdriver

the nun could have backed you up

the nun in black & white
sits apart from her children
like legs open for sex

the schoolkid's lips/breasts/& hips
i smile at the word kid
she's no kid

some of the sand had to be removed from under the feet of the
shadows, so as to allow them to swing freely without touching

to those areas that
on subject to im-
and other differences
, their lifestyles and
diversity, there is a
ormity – in part
om the interaction
f family and home
within australianism itself

of australian ways of thinking
views of australian women.
, beach, car and
nunciation, purity,
d structural categ-
female stereotypes
wife, honoured
owerful, sexual part-
nts in the context

s that of the fridge
ng of three inter-
estruction – with
en, nurturant mother
os has demonstrated
he metaphysical, but
out that each of
when restricted to
the final section i
can, in their positive
extreme positions
cture of goals can be
tween the renouncer
un be alternately
uctive, ally/opponent

attention on the more
ut women. i make no
and behaviour, a task

*put the gun down. put the gun down now. put the gun down. in the
shop, put your gun down and come out straight away. we can see you.
put the gun down. put the gun down and come straight through the
door. put the gun down. put the gun down and come straight out.
now. we have had enough*

P – O – W – E – R

spells power

the power trip ship

        of the oldies foldies

                *over this that other brand
of use by now young*

the mathematical equation of

                put them down/keep them in their place

        behind the wall of their skin

           their fingers are mad dog cans of air

                    4 fingers and a thumb
                                        are dangerous in the wrong hands
        the call of the wild wall
                            the a-wrong-utang eye
                that converts brick veneer to the romance of chaos
                that dark romance
                                    that secret breath
                                                    of the sea
            that's still in us
                        that wants to spray-can the fence-line in us
                                            with breakers
                that crash against the grain
                                    of our bank solid rock state

        prison walls
                        to keep us inside the real estate rationalisation
            of real estate time
                            police prices
                                        the mercantile whirl wheel
            of buy consume buy sell the worship of the religious art of the thing
                you are a thing
                i am a thing
                                    you are invalid invalid . . . dot dot dot
i'm going to punch you out
                        the ticket of your eyes
        if you do not say obey
                            the realisation of me as power trip
along the track of your handcuffed tongue
                come on sorry sonny but
        it's my orgasm here and now
                        art is the eye of the beholder
        and i am the power of the beholder of nice
                                            brick
        with more power
                        to wash your mouth out
                                            with b.o.-less paint
            laubmans berger breeze the niceness of a nice soft pastel
        nothing too loud
                        no dissidence

N – O

is the capitalisation of no

straight lines. tracks. streets

straight hands

N – O

art is not leonardo's last supper

of you on a wall consuming us, thank you, but

art is not aboriginal

it is the rock art of money money money

the art of making more

1 million dollars to clean you off us

and keep you kitchen-tidy

S.A. great, mate

cleanliness is next to godliness

cleanliness is the hospitalised wall

don't think back beyond the art of the laundromat wall

no identity other than

corrugated iron brick

plastic leather weather

seats are for bums

not question marks

not altered states

of consciousness run riot

we know our destination

straight through through through

the city of the straight line

is the art of the capitalised city

capital – ism – elitism

eatism

legal   ill & legal

legal & ill

(sounds like a firm of lawyers i know)

politicians are legal

pretty polly wants a cracker

pay-rise cracker

don't break the art of the law

is   -litism   eatism

rightism

we are right you are wrong(-ism)
the left fare left far behind
and out of sight, man, keep out of sight
you think   we think
you be   we be
us
all together (in one)
us only
OUR AESTHETICS your aesthetics
OUR LOVE your love
love our decor
or else
buddy boy
for we are the end of your beginning
believe me
you are us   lump it
or there's no ticket to ride

U – N – E – M – P – L – O – Y – E – D

spells unemployed

what's that?
you definitely have an attitude problem, matey,
and we're going to wipe you off our wall with relish
and make you eat your words
slowly
make you believe in the mysterious way
of the street-sign lord
hallelujah
or else

we are us
and you are up against our wall
we have our eyes and minds pointed at YOU
move out of line
and you're HIT IT
believe me
BELIEVE ME
and what CHOICE do you really have

in the matter anyway?

the wall is your identity number
    so put your back up against it
        and file it away
            as we have

the leader of the party then made the following address to those present, viz.:-
    'shadows, this is the white's punishment for murder, the next time white men are killed in this country more punishment will be given. let none of you take these shadows down, they must hang till they fall in pieces. we are now friends, and will remain so, unless more white people are killed, when plenty more policemen will be sent to punish much more severely. all are forgiven except those who actually killed the wrecked people, who, if caught, will also be hung. you may now go, but remember this day, and tell what you have seen to the others'

    beneath monroe's kiss/her face/her look
    we eye each other off while dribbling wine & air

    the camera circling/4 walls/not the 3 of theatre/
        the body

    the sea & overblown faces in the background

    framed in doorways/
        pain

    put the gun down. walk out through the doorway. we're not going to hurt you. we have had enough. walk through the door. put the gun down. put the gun on the floor. come through the doorway. leave the gun inside. we want you to come out the shop now. leave the gun inside

    it beats its wings into emotion

    ideologies above the road edge
    its eyes are invisible

its body is totalitarian

soft death is steel. the heart
is the mouse thing
it constructs out of the smoke and web
of its pity

it punctuates full stops
like a boulder from the sky.
it is grammar

lethal and archaic
it forces its way through the machinery of air
to its tree on the horizon.
a vertical in the abstract

it rests there

its eyes simmer

*the shadows, whose hands had been unbound after the execution,
bolted off, and disappeared like magic. we then started back and
reached the camp in the evening, where three or four men had been left
in charge*

in the office/in the office/in the office
money money money
mother mother mother
wife son wife son
the snow sets around us
when there is no snow
   actors with the same name as reality
   light a candle in a candlestick
& wipe out a family & neighbour with blows
  while watching t.v.
  then you wipe yourself out by hanging yourself in
      a toilet with your own tie/
  let them break in a toilet door
  if they want your body
  & a shit in peace/away from the office

& corridors

hire-purchase sex/the bailiff comes
around to take your wife back/
working towards a breakdown in a train station
so you can keep your wife & 'free' sex/
killing the barman because he looks like your father/
acts like your father/
& you can't ask him for money/rob him
so you can keep your wife
& hire-purchase sex/
can you wave goodbye to the furniture
& your wife
without a feeling of failure?
be content with sex-magazines?

*do not come out with the gun. i repeat, do not come out with the gun.
in the shop, put your gun down and walk through the doorway. we
have had enough*

winds wind down and fall and shatter

asphalt crawls and lies to shadows

pipelines move and catch at feet

whispers predominate. executives lunch

food coughs and suits die

glass cries and people consume it

hands run and windows listen

trees talk. we are all outsiders

tongues perch and clouds lick

paper is poison and bodies respond

ledges are birds and feathers heavy

performance is relative. the wardrobe wins

typewriters are phones and the word gets out

letters are drinkers and the word gets in

performance is passion and the sky shouts

the traffic laughs. people colour

the air is human and nothing is left

in some shelters of the shadows we found more European clothing
stained with blood and a silver watch. the shelters were set on fire, and
their contents burnt; the watch, however, was preserved and brought
back to the city with us

rain is only a temporary compromise

drizzle saws at my face

cars are driven like religious fists
no art in their survival
only grit and iron prayer
bare-knuckle

they swear at the air   yank distance at their eyes
swerve through

i catch some sounds
prise their legs off
drop them inconsequentially to the ground
(ground)   grind my shoes

everything mutters

my legs talk back to themselves

slowly we leak
towards a compromise
and effort becomes a hole
that connects me to the rain

i turn around
to see what i've mist
when the rain lets up
– only a stain on the landscape

we'll do something about it. if you have a complaint about someone
else we'll do something about it. talk to us. we'll do something about it
if you had a problem with somebody yesterday. do you understand?
come on out. come on out. put the gun down

claire
in writing about a humour called a raddit
has left us without an explanation
of its habit

that being so
does it eat backwards?

do lettuces sprout from its mouth
to be nibbled by the ground?

does it make burrows in the air
and run along invisible corridors
for all of us to stare?

does a white tail grow
from its nose?

do its front paws
spring from its back
and tip it forward on its nose, 'er tail
when it sits gazing around
at some dream in its head? of chasing dogs, maybe,
back into kennels?

does it say 'what's down . . . .'
instead of 'what's up, doc?'
and secretly replant carrots at night
in elmer fudd's already over-stocked carrot patch
much to his surprise?

and does it does does does it
does it eat humans?
and wear their skins as coats
during winter?

it had been raining all day and i looked about for a dry place.
observing a large hole in the bank of the creek, i crept into it, lay
down, and soon fell in a sound sleep but when the men saw me emerge
there was great laughter: it appeared that one of the troopers had been
watching with his loaded carbine for an animal at the same hole for
some hours, with the intention of firing into it if he heard the least
noise. fortunately, however, my undisturbed sleep saved me from a bullet

wa(r)ter is a promiscuous hand. the promised land.
wa(r)ter lies on the asphalt like a wet tongue's footprint.
the sky is a grind of metal on metal. the crush is wa(r)ter
on wa(r)ter. gradually the sky melts into eyes that fall hard
onto edges. the walls between the hands. the fingertips
that hang onto the footholds between the ground and the sky.
r weather. things r rain(s). hard r rain(s).
the landscape is (a) hard rain. the landscape is (a) scrape escape.
hard rape. wa(r)ter wa(r)ter everywhere and not a drop to think.
this is the way the brain rains not with a bang but a.
the sailor ses the wa(r)ter is. the soldier ses the wa(r)ter is.
the airman ses the wa(r)ter is. the egg that breaks between the testicles
and the act of irruption. take the egg and run.
humpty dumpt is a dirty old man. last one home is a rotten old egg.
the mouth is a wide-open 0 that takes in molecules in preparation
for the act of solitude. wa(r)ter is the tough edge of the wedge.
it is the weather of the ego edgo that falls from the robot's eye.
camera-in-the-sky. they lie. we die. the metal in the wa(r)ter.
the metal is the wa(r)ter. heavenly wa(r)ter. let us make-believe.
like metal in the wa(r)ter we reflect the cloud in the machine.
r coin. rcane

put the gun down. come through the door. come to the door. we
won't hurt you. come to the door. put the gun down. put the gun
down. put the gun down on the ground. put it down. put the gun down
and talk to us

eating rosalie & graham
    & chasing the independence of australia
    like a dog chasing its cliché/
    preferring to live in america/
    more money/people/& influence/
    american cinema almost destroyed german cinema in the 50s/
    the woman of the letter saying hullo to rosalie/
    her wax smooth face/no look at me

            /i have my coke & a packet of chips.
            paranoia is such
                a delicate pleasure
&
    as i sit
        & eat
   amongst the sts. in the car
i watch a rain drop/the windscreen is in decline
                        &
                          fall

and i contend, that in all circumstances of wholesale murder by
shadows, such as in the circumstance of the wreck, summary justice is
the best preventive against the repetition of crime, and is more likely,
by striking terror at once, to get at the truth of events, than a tedious
process of law. subsequent occurrences have confirmed this opinion

    they moved in on the sky first
    pulling out the nails holding down the blue sheets
    and without a sideways glance hurled them over the side

    they didn't even flinch at the thundering crash
    and the rafters of red were the next in line

    everything was retreating downwards now
    step by step

    and the hills were the next to go
    knocked down with a few judicious taps in the right places
    then shovelled into a truck and carted away

everybody was now back to ground level
and becoming concerned

then after the dust had settled
they moved in on the river and pulled the plug

everyone was suffocating
– squeezed together along the bottom line
the last line of defence

and the foreground
having little fight left in it
was quickly swept over the edge with a deft flick or two

it was then that they knocked off
and in step shuffled backwards out of time

they didn't have far to go

Wakefield Press is an independent publishing and
distribution company based in Adelaide, South Australia.
We love good stories and publish beautiful books.
To see our full range of titles, please visit our website at
www.wakefieldpress.com.au.